Considerations for the City Dog

Melissa McCue-McGrath, CPDT-KA

Publisher: MuttStuff Publishing

Editors: Judith Kurtz Bogdanove, Leah H. Tremble, Kenneth Mallon

General Editor: Brian McGrath

Cover photos taken by Dave Harmin (Print version) &
Ron Mesard (e-Book version)

ISBN: 978-0-9962755-0-7

1. Pets 2. Education

First Edition

Printed in the United States

This book would not exist if it weren't for my inquisitive students and the exuberant dogs that they love.

This book would not exist without my friends, colleagues, students and family who donated their works, their photos, their editorial skills, their time and their enthusiasm to help me see this book all the way through to completion.

This book would not exist if my two-year-old daughter failed to keep a regimented nap schedule for two hours, every day.

Most of all, it wouldn't exist without Sadie-Jane.

Table of Contents

Introduction

Over the last ten years working as a dog trainer in Boston, I've noticed a pattern. Students understandably want classes that address the how-to's or *verbs* of training their dogs, like how to get them to sit, stay, stop jumping on kids, and play fetch. These skills are really important, and I feel strongly that all pet dogs should have some basic skills. There are already thousands of books to help with these key skills on the market.

This is not one of those books.

Instead, this book encompasses the questions we trainers get asked on a daily basis that really ought to be addressed more comprehensively than we are able or qualified to answer in a class setting.

- "How do I find a reputable breeder?"
- "My adult dog needs to be socialized. Should I bring him to daycare?"
- "Should I bring my puppy to the dog park?"
- "She's pulling so hard on walks. What walking device should I use?"
- "My dog won't walk at all. What do I do?"
- "Should I spay my dog?"
- "My dog barks when I'm gone. Does he have separation anxiety?"
- "Are you a behaviorist?"
- "What's this rash? Should I see a vet?" (Yes. Now.)

We see the entire relationship. We see the little things that make the relationship work, or completely break the relationship down. We also see breaches of dog owner etiquette every day and more often than not, these breaches are unintentional. When dog professionals hang out, we often talk about "that guy." You may even know him:

- That Guy who has a dog that aggressively barks at everyone from behind a fence or a window. All. Day. Long;
- That Guy who lets his dog walk down the street without a leash, while we watch it almost get hit by a car;
- That Guy who yells "It's ok! He's friendly!";
- That Guy who uses a retractable leash and prong collar in the dog park;
- That Guy whose dog frequently jumps the fence;
- That Guy who leaves his dog in a hot car, "only for a minute";
- That Guy who lets his aggressive dog play at the dog park;
- That Guy who ignores pleas for space with the excuse "It's OK. I love

dogs!";

- That Guy who has done everything right, but his dog reacts aggressively on walks (we feel bad for this guy);
- That Guy with a Harley, badass tattoos, and a Maltese named "Cupcake" (He doesn't have a problem, we just love this guy).

The issues that arise from these breaches come up in conversation whenever two or more owners or dog professionals get together. Sometimes common, preventable issues result in unintended stress to a family, neighbors and members of the community.

There's no doubt in my mind that most owners are well-intentioned. It's really hard to have a dog in the city with eight-hour work days, neighbors six feet away, and skateboards whizzing by on city streets. They just don't know where to go to learn the other critical skills that aren't covered in basic training classes.

I wrote this book after working for over a decade with trainers through various dog training clubs, centers and facilities. I'd hear the same issues come up again and again on both sides of the client/trainer relationship. I would field the same questions in every single class. It dawned on me that I could, and probably should, write a useful handbook that can be used in tandem with any positive reinforcement training class. I thought it would be a good idea to discuss these common issues and direct owners to the appropriate professionals, while also giving my fellow dog trainers a resource guide, so they can focus on the verbs of dog training again.

I thought about it for a while but always had an excuse. I didn't have time to write. I didn't think anyone would buy the book. I had a baby. I didn't think that I'd be able to effectively get across all the little things that can really help all dogs, not just dogs in the city. I have a blog that I don't edit particularly well, because it's *a blog*. There are so many other books on the market that are written by people way more qualified than little-old-me. I have to check Facebook just *one more time*.

Then, in November 2013, a dog in my city nearly killed a 6'4" man and his German shepherd. Everyone came out of the woodwork with their expert opinions on how to handle matters.

- Euthanize the dog.
- Save the dog.
- He needs more training.
- He needs a muzzle.
- He needs love.
- Fire the Animal Control Officer.
- The Animal Control Officer is doing a good job.
- There are no bad dogs, only bad owners.
- The owner is a terrible person for letting this happen.
- It's Obama's fault!
- Cats are better.

When that happened, I knew I had to do something. Out of that tragedy, *Considerations for the City Dog* was born.

This is my attempt to help dogs and their owners find reputable resources to address small annoyances before they result in a terrible incident (like the one in my city). Although, I would argue everything in this book is important for all dogs, regardless of location, special attention should be paid to our urban hounds because of the unique stressors they face every single day.

In writing this, I consulted with trusted veterinarians, dog owners, certified dog trainers, dog-walkers, doggie daycare providers, groomers, previous students, animal control, rescue volunteers and behavior consultants to find the common missteps they wish they'd avoided with their own dogs, or issues they see with enough frequency with their clientele that they needed to be noted. These are the things they want to say to every dog owner out there, which, interestingly, line up with the issues I see in my own work. If professionals in several dog-related industries are seeing similar issues, I would argue that this is indicative of something not working. We owe it to our dogs to know where they are coming from (literally and figuratively), what they need, and how to make their lives better in light of leash laws and barking ordinances. We owe it to our neighbors who might not love dogs as much as we do, because in cities we all share the same space.

I sincerely hope this book can help head off common issues and frustrations we see in our busier environments while providing dog owners the best possible chance of being successful with their four-legged friends. We can all live comfortably and happily with our dogs, in our communities and in our cities. We just need to do a few things to make sure we are all doing right by our dogs.

Lastly, in the interest of full disclosure, I have made many of the mistakes outlined in this book and was *that guy* with my own dogs, so no judgments here. I am human (just like you) and that was probably the worst possible thing for my dogs.

Luckily for me, they were dogs, so they obviously forgave me.

Dogs rule.

~Melissa McCue-McGrath, CPDT-KA
APDT #774549

Choosing the City Dog

Bigger isn't always better, and smaller isn't always city-friendly

As we started selecting traits in dogs for hunting, retrieving, herding, ratting and guarding, we stumbled onto a bond that has been unbreakable for over 10,000 years. Through fields, frontiers and urban centers, our best friends have always been right there with us, every step of the way.

Mason is a 4 1/2 year old, boxer/hound mix.
He enjoys howling, chasing squirrels, and hogging the bed.
Photo submitted by Jaime & Evan DaSilva, Charlestown, MA

There are many things to consider when selecting a new pet. The first question shouldn't be "How do I get a dog?" Instead, make this easier for yourself in the long run and figure out why you want a dog. Do you want a running partner, a hiking buddy, a dog you can take everywhere with you, or do you want a dog because you just like dogs? Do you want a companion to curl up with you at night? Did you grow up with dogs, or is this your first foray into pet ownership?

For starters, look at the different groups of dogs. The American Kennel Club (AKC) divides dogs into seven groups (I add two more) and within each group are dozens of specific breeds, traits, and drives.

- **Terriers:** Most of these dogs descended from ratters and vermin hunters. They were bred to seek out problem critters ranging from rats to badgers. I would argue we need more rat terriers in my city, but that's a different tangent! Dachshunds were bred to dive head-first into badger holes, grab the vermin by the face, and pull it out to be exterminated.

That's a tough little dog! The common traits typically seen in all terriers include tenacity, independence, and self-confidence. They tend to have higher prey drive than some other dogs and need a lot more exercise than most owners would typically expect.

- **Sporting Dogs:** These are dogs that should be engaged in some sort of activity like swimming, running, or fetch in the back yard. In this group are dogs that retrieve, like the golden retriever; dogs that flush birds out of brush, like the English springer spaniel; and dogs that point out game, like the English pointer and the Irish setter. These dogs need to run and be worked, and most of them tend to make their owners laugh every single day.

- **Herding Dogs**: These are dogs that typically need more exercise than marathon runners, and are typically smarter than Mensa students. These dogs move sheep, cattle, goats, and if you aren't careful, children. The Border collie, Belgian Malinois, Australian shepherd (which is an American breed!) and Pembroke Welsh corgi are all examples of herding dogs. Training and extracurricular activities are an absolute must for most herding dogs.

- **Toy Dogs:** Toys are wee-little dogs that were bred to be companions, foot warmers, and security alarm systems. Many smaller breeds wake at the drop of a hat, so the little yappy bark was bred into some of these dogs at just the right pitch to wake the bigger, tougher, lumbering guard dogs. Others were bred to be foot warmers and social companions. The Maltese, pug, and Chihuahua are some of the more popular toy breeds.

- **Hounds:** The hound group can be divided into scent hounds and sight hounds. Scent hounds, like the beagle and bloodhound, are the dogs that always have their noses to earth, taking in every scent molecule. Sight hounds are the dogs that chase down prey at high speeds, like the greyhound and Irish wolfhound.

- **Working Dogs:** These are the all-purpose, strong, and high-endurance dogs that pull carts, guard property, and watch over livestock. An example of this is the Great Pyrenees. If it looks like a sheep, acts like a sheep, and barks *unlike* a sheep, it's probably a Pyr. This rather large, white dog is literally raised with a flock of sheep. It blends in with the sheep and protects the flock. If a coyote or trespasser threatens the woolen brethren, the Pyr comes out of hiding, defends the flock, and usually wins.

- **Non-Sporting Dogs:** This group is the least consistent. These are the dogs that are not in any of the other groups. When the AKC originated in 1884, dogs were classed as either sporting or non-sporting. The herding and working dogs split out of the sporting category; the toy dogs and terriers split out of the non-sporting category, and the hounds were lumped together. The non-sporting category is virtually all that is left. In the United Kennel Club (UKC), this is called the *miscellaneous category*. In this group are dogs like the Xoloitzcuintli (*show-low* for short) which is a hairless Mexican dog, and the better-known Dalmatian.

- **Designer Dogs:** These dogs have recent ancestors of two different breeds. Unlike the Great Dane, which is a distinct breed that descended from mastiffs and greyhounds centuries ago, designer breeds are not recognized by national breed groups…yet. Some of these crosses are fantastic dogs that have seeped into the zeitgeist, like the *labradoodle* (descendants of both Labradors and poodles), the *cavapoo* (Cavalier King Charles spaniel and poodle) and the *bogle* (Boston terrier and beagle). The theory I hear more than any other is that these dogs get the best qualities of each breed, and none of the undesirable qualities, but genetics don't work that way! If you have one of these dogs in mind, make certain that you are getting one from a well-researched breeder as discussed in the next chapter, just as you would a purebred dog.

- **Mutts and Crosses (Heinz 57):** Dogs that have a mystery basket of traits and personality! Some are related to purebred dogs, while others have never had a known breed in their lineage. Like all of the dogs above, these are individuals who have distinct needs and drives.

It's a good idea to start asking lifestyle questions regarding any hypothetical dog in the home. Who will walk the dog? Where will the dog sleep? Is anyone allergic? Is there a preference for male or female dogs in the household? What is the annual budget, including vet bills, food, toys, unexpected surgery, day care, boarding, and other expenses? Is there a particular look you are attracted to? Also consider that if you have a big family or want kids, getting a dog that is amenable to changing scenery, an active lifestyle, and is trainable is a great place to start.

After all of those questions are answered, there are a few additional considerations when a dog is going to live in an urban environment. For starters, small size does not immediately qualify a dog to live in an apartment; there are dozens of small dog breeds that require hours of outdoor activity, like the Jack Russell terrier. Believe it or not, many of the small dog breeds, like the American Eskimo dog, were originally bred to be watchdogs. Watchdogs tend to be incredibly sensitive to noises, and prefer to alert bark when things are in motion, which might make living in a noisy apartment building intolerable for the dog, for the family, and for neighbors. The beagle, though a sweet natured companion, is notorious for "the beagle bark"; a mournful baying vocalization that was bred into the beagle to alert hunters that game has been located. Your neighbors may not appreciate centuries of careful breeding and instinctive howling as much as you do. Though many dogs of these breeds do well in the city individually, each breed has traits to consider before introducing them into any environment, but specifically urban ones.

"We want to play with those kids!"
Elvis (Border collie) and Britney (whippet) in Somerville, Massachusetts
Photo by Andy Winther

What was your dog bred to do?

German shepherds are beautiful dogs, are highly trainable, and consistently rank among the top five smartest dog breeds; however, with that intelligence comes great responsibility. These dogs were bred to be an all-purpose herding and guarding dog. They can be a great family pet, but shepherds who are looking for a job to do and aren't mentally stimulated enough will often get themselves into trouble by barking at every noise they pick up with their superior hearing. They are also known to develop sensitivities to anything that is different in their environment, thanks to their guarding history. In an urban setting, pretty much everything is part of a changing environment. Some of these genetic behaviors are difficult to manage in the city, unless you are engaged in sports and a daily training regimen on top of the hours of aerobic activity necessary for young shepherds.

On the other hand, if you want a hiking buddy, a French bulldog might not be your best bet, unless you just want a dog to keep the sofa warm while you take off on solo-hikes! These dogs can be sensitive to fluctuating temperatures because they are brachycephalic, or have a smooshed-in face. This makes regulating their internal temperature difficult. They can also be quite expensive. These dogs have been bred to the point where they wouldn't exist in nature as they are currently. For the most part, bulldog and French bulldog puppies are conceived via artificial insemination because their bodies aren't able to fit together for the mating event without human intervention. Frenchie inseminator is not a job that I personally want on my résumé. Additionally, the heads of the puppies are too big to fit through the birth canal, so cesarean section is now fairly standard in bulldog and French bulldog births. All of this is included in the cost of your puppy.

What is your current daily routine? Consider both work and play!

On average, Americans work eight-hour days, and commutes can be painfully long. That has to be figured into the amount of time Fido will be left alone. Ten hours daily without anyone around is a long time for a dog, or any social animal. There are dog-walkers, park playgroups, doggie daycares, and other options for city-dwelling dogs (more on this later), but they are not appropriate options for every pooch. This absolutely has to be factored into the equation before choosing the right pet for you, regardless of whether you live in the city or not.

In addition to what your dog will do while you're working, consider the activities you would like to do with your new canine companion when you're together, and make sure that those activities are realistic. If you have never run a mile in your life but you want a running companion, you might want to give running a try for 30 days prior to selecting a dog. You might really love running, which means a high-drive dog might be a great fit, or you might really hate running, which means your running partner needs a lot more activity than you are able to provide. Think about your daily routine as it stands currently and see what type of dog would likely suit the activities that you are already engaged in, instead of using your dog as a motivational tool to do activities that typically aren't part of your daily agenda.

What floor do you live on?

Do you want to help a 200 pound mastiff up and down the stairs to the fifth floor apartment if he is unable to get up and down the stairs due to arthritis, or an accident? What if your dog is sick and you can't lift him down the stairs? Unless your job is professional weight lifter, weight should be at least a moderate consideration.

"Where am I supposed to pee? What is all this cold white stuff?"
Huxley, a 10 week old Australian shepherd puppy, is owned by
Alyson and Matt Deutsch of Charlestown, MA

Secondly, I speak from experience: Potty training a puppy from the third floor is not a joy ride. When the puppy starts to pee inappropriately, owners tend to grab the puppy and take it outside. If you happen to live on any higher level in an apartment building, the mad race down the back stairs is an adventure worthy of Benny Hill's theme song. Imagine a scene where the puppy is squirming, and puppy pee is trickling down your arm while you quickly stutter step down each creaking stair. You struggle to open the back door. All the while, you're pleading with the puppy to "just hold it," and swearing under your breath like a pirate. When you finally open the door to the sweet, smoggy city air, you have a puppy with an empty bladder, who now just wants to play outside.

Pee pads are an option for many high rise city dwellers for the reason detailed above, but to reiterate, a small Chihuahua using pee pads is something that most people can clean up and accept in their home. The mastiff using pee pads would be a less acceptable long-term solution. Though they do make pee pads that size, you'd likely want to buy stock in tarp. This might not be an acceptable option if you ever want company to visit.

What is the age of the dog?

Puppies require a lot of individualized attention. In the beginning they need to go out at least once or twice an hour, every hour. As a general rule, their bladders are not physically able to "hold it" for longer periods during waking hours. The bladder is a muscle, and like all muscles it takes time to build strength. If you plan on having your puppy alone for eight hours at a time while you're at work, a puppy is likely not going to be an appropriate match for you. If you insist on getting a puppy and work all day away from home, you will have to invest in a dog-walker, neighbor, or caretaker to let the puppy out several times a day, which can get expensive. If you work from home, set your alarm every 60 minutes to take the puppy out for a break, even if you are on an important phone call.

Senior dogs also need to go out much more frequently. As dogs age, they can have a harder time "holding it." Asking a 12-year-old dog with arthritis to stay alone for eight hours without a break is really unfair. Get a dog-walker or a neighbor to let your aging dog out for breaks through the day while you are working.

Are there apartment or condo size restrictions on resident dogs?

You found the perfect companion for you—a beautiful, happy, 75-pound lab mix from the shelter that you can take jogging. He loves people, loves dogs, and isn't too jumpy. It's too bad that your lease specifies dogs under 25 pounds, and it's not negotiable per your landlord. It's critical that you know the rules and regulations of the apartment or condo before you go looking for your new best friend.

Riley is a retired racing greyhound. When he's not sound asleep on a sofa, he is traveling with his best friend, Ron Mesard of Somerville.

There are cities in Massachusetts in which there is a three-dog maximum, including resident and boarded dogs. Breeders, foster owners, and service providers need to get special permits to have more than three dogs on the property overnight. Contrast that with Maine: when I was growing up, we had a dog sledding team, so we legally had ten dogs on our property. Make sure that you are aware of city and state regulations in addition to the rules listed on your lease to avoid fines, eviction, or having to re-home your new dog.

Keep an open mind!

Most people think that greyhounds are really fast dogs with an insatiable appetite for running. This is absolutely not the case for most greys. They are often called "the 40 miles per hour couch potato" for a reason! After living with one that slept more hours a day than an average house cat, I would have to agree. I've also met one greyhound that is more energetic than my Border collie. There are breed characteristics for all breeds, but within that breed is great variety.

You may have an idea about a particular look of dog or a breed, but without keeping an open mind you could be missing out on the perfect dog for your lifestyle. While a greyhound might not be the best type of dog for someone who wants a jogging partner, that same dog might be a lovely companion for most on-the-go city slickers (plus, they are the perfect arm candy!) Conversely, Boston terriers are sturdy little dogs and tend to be higher energy than expected. Some like to run as long as it's not too hot or too cold outside. They can be great option for a more active family in the city.

Are there breed bans or lease restrictions for the type of dog want?

Breed bans are popping up all over the country. Usually they are restricted to a county or city, but many landlords are also writing breed bans into leases. Depending on the law in each locale, if your dog is muzzled at all times on the premises, or if you pass the Canine Good Citizen Test (CGC), your dog might be able to stay. Some communities have outright bans on certain types of dogs, so those dogs can't live in certain locations, no matter what paperwork you have.

Regardless of whether or not these laws are fair (they aren't), they continue to exist. Many home insurance companies will not cover you if you have a specific breed or mix. Again, fairness aside, these clauses are written into policies. As a result, some shelters and rescue groups are not forthcoming, or genuinely don't know the types of dogs they are homing. If you don't know much about dogs, you could be taking a lab-mix home, only to later find out that he's a banned breed. This has happened to a few of my students, and they've had to jump through a lot of unfair hoops to keep their beloved pets.

I once had a student who was told she was getting a Labrador/boxer mix from a rescue group. All the paperwork said "lab/boxer." She had the dog for a couple of weeks when she came to our training facility. My boss asked me to meet the dog and tell her what breed I thought it was. What she had was a 35-pound, muscular, wiggly, affectionate Staffordshire terrier—a breed banned by her homeowners' insurance. This particular dog helped her autistic son come out of his shell, become more social, and even helped him participate in my canine disc class. Watching that dog and that boy was pure joy. That dog was absolutely the best thing for this family. However, because she was in the category of what most people would recognize as a pit bull, they were at risk of losing their homeowners' insurance, even though the paperwork said "lab/boxer."

This isn't the only case of banned breeds I've had in classes, and every time it happens to a well-intending, fantastic family and their equally fantastic dog, I can't help but get worked up at the injustice of it all. Pit bulls and bully breeds (umbrella terms for dogs that tend to have a blocky head and muscular body), though often very sweet and affectionate, are the main target of breed bans and breed-specific legislation (BSL). Meanwhile, I had an Irish setter bite his owner after the dog attacked a shrinking-violet bull mastiff in my class. The mastiff just turned around and took the setter's abuse until the setter's owner pulled him off, and that's when he got bitten in the bicep. Personality matters, not breed. That mastiff could have been on mandatory muzzle order, and the Irish setter's owner still would have been bitten by his own dog, because the problem isn't mastiffs, pit bulls or any other type of dog. The problem is sometimes bad training practices, inappropriate settings for particular dogs, or not knowing realistically what an individual dog can handle.

Lilah at the Beach
Photo by Torrie Dwyer

Everywhere you turn, the consensus is "There are no bad dogs, just bad owners," and while that's sometimes the case, sometimes the dog is not placed in an appropriate environment, or sometimes a dog genetically can't cope around strangers. Sometimes it's the dog, sometimes it's the owner, sometimes it's the environment, and sometimes it's a combination of everything. It's complicated. It is not a breed or phenotype of animal. It's genetics, personality, people, environment, health, training and specific situations.

Many cities are wise to the fact that BSL and breed bans don't work effectively to protect people. Dogs as individuals need to be considered dangerous or friendly, instead of banning entire breeds, or types of dogs. What's worse is there are dogs that might look a certain way, even if they are a mixed breed of unknown origin that can still get caught in the breed ban umbrella. Be cognizant of the dog you are getting, and if you don't know, bring a professional with you. A certified professional can give a broad idea of what the likely exercise requirements are, and let you know if you are at risk of bringing a banned breed of dog into your home. Be aware of the restrictions in your city, community, building, or homeowners insurance before getting a dog, so you don't have to move, lose your insurance policy or worse—lose your dog because she happens to be a banned breed.

I usually say the breed doesn't matter as much as temperament, but when it comes to BSL and insurance policies, I've seen some hearts broken. If you plan on owning a husky, which is a banned dog in some homeowners' insurance policies and communities, make sure you have an apartment outside of that jurisdiction. Better yet, organize a petition, get lawmakers on your side, and bring attention to the issue. These bans will exist as long as there is misinformation about dog breeds and bans being "successful" (again, they aren't). The more people who advocate eliminating these bans in these jurisdictions, and elect officials who don't support breed bans, the better off our dogs will be.

Malachi is the proud owner of Michelle and Paul Acciavatti.
He would have left his graffiti tag, but he doesn't have thumbs.

We have evolved with dogs by our side for 10,000 years. We have moved from village to frontier, frontier to farm, and farm to city, and our dogs have come with us every step of the way. With more dogs moving into urban centers that have very specific needs due to breeding and genetics, we owe it to them to make sure that we are doing everything to pay homage to their specific needs and sensitivities. They give up a lot to live with us. When they live in cities they are giving up freedom, outlets, exploration and the lull of a quiet night, all for our partnership and the safety we provide. We owe it to them to take them as individuals and do everything in our power to do right by our dogs, because they just don't have a say in the matter. The best way to give them what they need is to be totally honest with ourselves as to what any individual dog should be asked to handle in this partnership, because for many of our dogs, they are getting the short end of the stick.

Considerations for a Dog Budget

<u>Initial Costs</u>:
- Cost of the dog
  - Pounds, shelters and rescues range from $50 - $500
  - Purebred dogs typically are $600 to $2500 (or more) from a well-researched breeder as discussed in the next chapter.
- Food dishes and a food bin
- Dog food: Many commercial dog foods have fillers while some others have too much protein. According to Dr. Nicholas Dodman at Tufts University[1], many of our dogs have way too much protein in their diet. Adult dogs require 18% protein in their food, yet many dog foods are marketing 30% protein, or more. Talk with your vet to determine a good food for your particular pet.
- Puzzle toys and other toys for the new dog
- Dog bed
- Crate (big enough to stand up and turn around in comfortably)
- Leash, collar for ID tags, and any other walking equipment
- Poop bags
- Dog brush, nail clippers, and a first aid kit

<u>Medical Costs</u>:
- Initial exam from a vet: ASPCA averages $100-300 for a first visit.
- Spay or neuter: There are programs that allow for cheaper surgeries, but on average, $200-$500 for the surgery (anesthesia, in-hospital care, pain medication, pre-op blood work). If you got your dog from a shelter, this is typically included in the cost of your pet.
- Pet insurance: Monthly fee varies, though the ASPCA estimates average annual costs are around $225 a year. This is not covered in the book, but things unexpectedly happen. It's a great idea to research pet insurance options. They can reimburse you when the unexpected occurs, which it invariably will at some point. Ask any of your friends with dogs the scariest thing about having a dog and the story will always include, "We went to the emergency vet at 2am." If you don't want to get insurance, make sure you put money away for extra expenses like ear infections, limping, x-rays, and medications. If your dog is older, consider dentistry, surgery, and pain medication.

---

[1] Dodman NH, Reisner I, Shuster L, et al. *Effect of dietary protein content on behavior in dogs.* JAVMA 2000; 217:376-9

Emergencies without surgery can range from a few hundred dollars to $3,000+. With surgery, the cost goes up to $5,000 or more. If you think this is high, think about how much it costs a human to be in a hospital, and we have insurance. Insurance is there in case you need it, and when the unexpected happens, you will be glad you have it.

- Annual exam: The ASPCA assumes an average $250 annual exam fee, including rabies (required in all states). This is a national average and varies by area.
- Flea and tick treatments / Heartworm: As a pet's weight increases, the cost of medication to prevent fleas, tick borne illnesses and heartworm increases. Smaller dogs need a smaller budget for these monthly medications. You don't want Lyme, and you *really* don't want Heartworm, so these expenses are considered mandatory.

Owner-in-Absentia Costs:
- Daycare, dog-walker, or other daily exercise routine
- Boarding costs
- Shoes, boots, sweaters, couches, books, wallets and other miscellaneous items your dog will chew while you're gone!

Other Considerations:
- Dog training: Basic manners class in the Boston area averages $160-$225 for six weeks. Varies depending on region and facility.
- Sports classes: The cost of the class plus equipment. For example, canine disc is going to be cheaper than dog sledding because you only need sneakers and some flying plastic discs. To be successful in dog sledding, you need harnesses, snow, cold weather gear for you, cold weather gear for the dog, wax for the paws, at least two dogs, and a sled. Think critically about what you need for the class and the activity you are pursuing.
- Grooming: Average DIY bathing is $15-$25. If you have a long haired breed, or a dog that needs a professional groomer, the costs can range from $40 - $150 a groom (every six weeks, breed depending).

The love between two new friends?
Priceless.
(Aislyn and Bandito sharing a teething toy)

Breeders

How to find a reputable breeder and why it's important to do your research

Several times a week I consult on cases where a dog has found a loving home, but its needs still aren't being met. These are dogs that are coming from every possible situation imaginable. These are dogs that are coming from reputable breeders, rescues, shelters, truck stops, Craigslist, puppy mills and flown in from all over the country. The next two chapters will discuss what we trainers are seeing after the dog is homed. These chapters outline how to responsibly get a dog, what to avoid, and how to find the best option for you, regardless of what avenue you elect to take in your search for a family pet. Keep in mind that there are no guarantees when you are getting a dog, but there are things to look for to give you the best possible chance at getting a pet suitable for you. When you come to us, you would likely rather discuss "sit, down, and stay," instead of behavior modification medication and other tough subjects that most owners aren't signing up for when they are just looking for a trusty family companion.

Owners Stephen and Margie Weil have loved and adored all of the Leonbergers in their home, and seven-year-old Rosie is no exception. She's 152 pounds of love, fluff, drool, and spirit. If you can't handle the spit cloths, this isn't going to be the dog for you. If you do your homework, find a great breeder, and know the pros and cons of the breeds you are interested in, you will be as happy as the Weils…and your dog will be as happy as Rosie.

Breeder v. Shelter

There are days where my social media feed reads like a Supreme Court case, usually right after a televised dog show like Westminster. Several folks will chime in to support the AKC and other breed groups. The argument is that dog breeders are all lumped in under "bad breeders" and as a result we are at risk of losing quality dog breeds, if dog shows are banned or put under any new restrictions. Some vocal dog breed enthusiasts suggest that the shelters are money makers and are creating an industry of homeless pets for profit. Yikes—that sounds pretty terrible!

Rescue advocates defend shelters and rescues. They suggest that saving an animal is always better than adding to the overpopulation of unwanted dogs. That's hard to argue against, especially considering that there are between six and eight million dogs and cats in shelters. Half of those pets are euthanized each year. Those are difficult numbers to swallow. Additionally, rescue supporters point out that breed groups, such as the AKC, support poor breeding practices—including inbreeding—to promote a breed standard. As a result, they are breeding for exaggerated traits instead of personality, which is promoting unhealthy physical and behavioral traits in our domestic dogs.

What I've found in the last decade of dog training is that there is no right answer and that these might not be opposing viewpoints. Awesome dogs come from breeders and awesome dogs come from rescue groups. Behaviorally unsound and sick dogs can come from breeders, and also from rescue groups.

Those who want a unique breed of dog, have a particular fondness for a type of dog or want specific traits in a dog, might do very well going through a reputable breeder. Those who are interested in adopting dogs that are down on their luck will do well going through a reputable rescue agency or responsible shelter.

What isn't helpful is the constant arguing of "breeder vs. rescue" and what dog is "better." We can agree that all dogs deserve an environment in which they will thrive. Some will do better working on a farm, others will do great with a quiet family and others will enjoy city life.

The Elephant in the Room

The truth of the matter is that there are glaring issues with both the breeding industry and the rescue field, but it's not fair to paint either with a broad brush without first stating that there are beacons of light in each industry. There are fantastic individuals in each group of driven, knowledgeable, exemplary models for their particular vocation. There are excellent breeders who select for personality and select against common maladies that affect particular breed lines. There are amazing, hardworking rescue groups who genuinely care about placing dogs with families where they will thrive.

With that said…

On the whole, the breeding industry must do a better job of breeding out diseases and personality flaws when breeding for family life instead of breeding to a standard that encourages excessive deformities in many of our dog breeds. The AKC and breed groups should consult with reputable veterinarians to ensure the dogs being promoted as "healthy" are actually healthy specimens. Better yet, ethical veterinarians could judge the breed rings to prevent dogs like overweight Labradors and German shepherds with knocking knees. Pekingese that overheat from walking around a ring should not be lauded as well-bred, healthy dogs, but that is what happened in 2012 when a Pekingese named Malachy won Best-in-Show. This dog could not walk around the ring without requiring an ice pack after the event. The dogs that win these breed classes are the parents of the next generation of dogs, so if we are starting with unhealthy stock, even if they win a trophy at a nationally recognized dog show, those flawed genes are passed on to puppies that end up in homes and show rings. Potential owners need to know that just because a dog is registered with the AKC, the dog might not be a healthy specimen. Just because I register my car does not make me a safe driver.

On the other hand, shelters need to be more selective of dogs they can take in, so they can help those dogs to the best of their ability. They need to do a better job of conducting honest behavioral and physical evaluations in addition to improving breed classifications (including "no determinable breed," "Heinz 57" or "American Shelter Dog" if the primary breed type is unknown) on every dog to ensure that when a dog is placed, it's going to be a successful placement. They also must deny truck adoptions to get around state loopholes and have reliable resources for owners to contact after they bring a dog home. There should be a trial period to make sure that when a dog is placed, there is permission to bring it back if the relationship isn't working.

Both industries need to put a moratorium on shipping dogs directly to people. Rescues should partner with brick-and-mortar shelters or fostering groups, so people can see the dogs before making a decision to adopt. Reputable breeders need to put pressure on other breeding facilities to stop the shipment of dogs by plane, truck or other method, for profit. We all need to stand up and promote a very simple, ethical, responsible idea: potential dog owners should meet a dog, in person, prior to any decisions being made.

Regardless, it's up to you to do your homework. There are great breeders, great rescues and great shelters, but you just have to know what you're looking for.

Let's do this.

What Does "Reputable Breeder" Mean?
Thanks to the internet, it's really easy to find a puppy of any breed that can be shipped directly to you. Most people have heard the term *reputable breeder* and the overarching assumption is that if the dog wasn't from a pet store or a puppy mill, it's reputable enough. Pet stores, puppy mills and backyard breeders are all red-flag words that breeders don't want to be associated with, and over the last decade, all have lost favor as a means of acquiring dogs, at least on the surface. Many cities have banned the sales of puppies from pet stores in an attempt to cripple the puppy mill industry. Yet, the puppy mills continue to exist and are still thriving.

While pet stores are losing favor as a reliable method to get a puppy, internet sales on purebred dogs and designer-bred dogs have skyrocketed. Sometimes these are breeders who are breeding as a hobby, and everything works out just fine. But, sometimes these are puppy mills disguised as breeders who are using the internet to hide their inhumane practices. Puppy mills profit from sick and behaviorally unsound puppies. This is why it's imperative to always put your hands on the puppy first. It's so convenient to have a puppy shipped to you, but puppy mills survive because they bank on convenience. It's easy to ship a dog that isn't healthy, hide behind the internet, and say all the right things in order to make a sale. These breeders do not have the welfare of the puppy in mind. It's critical to meet the puppy first. Always.

However, even if you do put your hands on the dog you can find yourself in a situation that you are ill-prepared for. Holly* (name changed for privacy) is a long time student of mine. She and her husband were looking to find a new canine companion after the beloved family dog, Mac, suddenly passed away. These are two incredibly smart, capable, and accomplished people. They did their research, found a puppy that fit the qualifications they were looking for and drove out to Indiana to get their new puppy. They knew shipping wasn't advised. They wanted to reduce the likelihood of getting a puppy mill dog by going to the facility in person.

As soon as they drove up, they knew that they were at a puppy mill. Not being able to leave the puppy behind, they decided they would take the puppy anyway, bring him back with them to Massachusetts and figure it out later. Though puppy Gizmo is doing miles better than he was when I met him a few months ago, he still has little interest in snuggling or playing with the family in the way that they had hoped. This puppy can't be handled. He is terrified at the vet and is super-sensitive to touch, space, and new people in his environment. He has a hard time being in the vicinity of people, which makes teaching him basic commands like sit, down and stay nearly impossible. Luckily, the family has another dog, Zuul, who has been able to help take the lead. Though the new puppy will likely never be able to feel totally comfortable with people, he is, in my estimation, incredibly fortunate to have found this particular family.

The family is understandably frustrated and disappointed that the puppy is having a hard time—imagine how hard it would be for you to not be able to play with your own puppy. However, they have come to terms with how they have drastically improved Gizmo's life by just letting him be Gizmo and loving him for the dog he is. They work hard every day to help him come out of his shell, little by little, and they are doing an amazing job.

Puppy Gizmo and big brother, Zuul.
Keep in mind that 'adorable' is not permission to say hi. Gizmo's personal space bubble is big.
This difficult journey is one the entire family is now taking to help Gizmo feel comfortable around people. Zuul, however, could give zero cares about space, and will happily invade yours in return for kisses and belly rubs. He's helping Gizmo cope, and in return, gets a cuddle buddy, for life.

Now, before any judgment is passed, think about what you would realistically do in this situation. I very likely would have done the exact same thing, even though it's against everything I've been taught. Bad breeding outfits rely on people feeling bad for the dogs.

"He's sick and needs care. He needs help!"

"I feel awful! I can't leave him here. I can help him."

"She can't stay in that cage any longer."

Ideally, you shouldn't just be asking breeders if they are reputable in the same way you wouldn't ask a car salesman if he is reputable. You'd likely check review websites and ask friends where they got their cars, and then go to the dealer. This is why looking at the Better Business Bureau is a critical first step. Additionally, look at reputable breed groups and forums as well, to find people who have had great experiences in their search for a puppy.

Talk with local certified dog trainers. Ask if they know of breeders who are breeding for personality. I've seen many wonderful labradoodles come from great local breeders in my classes, and have had a few less-than-balanced labradoodles come from other breeders. There is one French bulldog breeder a few towns away whom I would recommend to anyone in the country. I would likely recommend the breeding facilities where I have seen dogs in my classes who are happy, social and are clearly matched appropriately to their owners. If a potential owner asked me if I knew of any dogs of any specific breed, I could reach out to my network of trainers, who would be able to recommend something personally.

Additionally, ask local veterinarians if they know of breeders they can recommend, since they may know which breeders locally are breeding healthy dogs. If they don't know of any specific breeders, they can, at the very least, help you determine what is considered a healthy physical trait. You can compare those good physical traits to the unhealthy, exaggerated traits that can lead to potential problems down the road. Be cautious about breeders who talk about how the long slope of a German shepherd's spine and crooked knees "help" the breed. Pugs with a flat face and double curled tail are more likely to have breathing issues, skin issues, and neurological issues than pugs whose faces aren't as pushed in, and those who aren't bred with a double curl in the tail[2].

Keep in mind that champion blood lines are not an indicator that a dog is healthy or behaviorally sound. It simply implies that the champion in

---

[2] *Pedigree Dogs Exposed.* Dir. Jemima Harrison. Passionate Productions. 2008. BBC One. Documentary. http://documentaryheaven.com/bbc-pedigree-dogs-exposed/

question won a beauty contest, and had enough training to behave in a chaotic show ring. Some champions are wonder-hounds and are amazing specimens, while some are just pretty enough to win a championship, but have exaggerated traits that are unhealthy. Do your research by going to breed shows, talking with qualified veterinarians, and really understand what exaggerated traits mean for the long-term health of dogs.

A qualified vet can also help you assess the medical issues that you should be prepared for with purebred dogs. For instance, some herding breeds suffer from collie-eye-anomaly, an inherited eye disease that can lead to blindness; greyhounds, unfortunately, suffer from higher instances of bone cancer; German shepherds are prone to hip dysplasia. These are all significant health issues that are common within particular breeds and groups. If the dog you choose ends up suffering from a breed-related illness, is it something that you can afford to fix, and emotionally cope with if the diagnosis is incurable?

It's important to know that a quality breeder will do several things. It might seem like you're jumping through hoops, but it's important to make sure that the dog you are paying a lot of money for is a quality dog, is behaviorally sound, and is physically sound. This breeder will make a client feel comfortable through the process by providing references and answering questions. A good breeder will likely have more questions for the potential owner than the other way around. Reputable breeders want to make sure that the puppy is going to a good family and a good environment. They want to know that the puppy they care for, the breed they love, is being well cared for in return.

There will be a contract outlining all of the expectations of the new owner, but also what the new owner can expect from the breeder. These contracts often include information about neutering and diet, although I prefer that any health considerations be made by a veterinarian and manners issues through a trainer. Additionally, they include what happens if the puppy gets sick in the first 14 days, and any potential diseases common in the breed. These contracts also include what happens if the dog needs to be re-homed. Most reputable breeders want to be looped into the conversation, or will even take the dog back at any age, for any reason. These breeders genuinely care about the dogs they breed, and that care doesn't diminish when the puppy leaves the premises.

If the contract seems too restrictive, for instance the puppy can only eat a particular brand of food or diet type for the rest of his life, or you can't have the dog neutered, ask if this is negotiable. It sounds wonderful if your new puppy is eating the very best quality food, but if you are a vegan and have a contract to feed your dog raw meat for the rest of his life, this might be too restrictive a contract. Raw might be a great option for a dog running the Iditarod, but maybe not the most appropriate option for a home with small children (salmonella) or for dogs that travel often (too much of a hassle).

Reputable breeders never just ship their puppies without meeting a potential owner prior to the sale. They insist that you meet on site, which is for your benefit as well as theirs. They want to make sure that their passion, these dogs they carefully breed, are going to responsible people. As a potential owner, you are looking to see that the kennels are clean. You are seeing firsthand that the puppies have been exposed to a variety of environments, dogs, and people. You are verifying that they were raised in a caring setting. The dogs should be friendly, healthy, and well cared for. Reputable breeders want you to see where the puppy comes from, because they take pride in what they do and they want to know that you care, too.

Beware of anyone who won't let you see the puppy in person, won't let you put your hands on the dog before purchasing, or uses phrases like "This is the last one, and she'll be gone by tomorrow." This isn't a breeder who is concerned about the welfare of the puppy or making a good match. This is a person more interested in making a sale.

Be wary of breeders who won't let you see the mother or other dogs on the premises. If the mother is anxious, aggressive, or highly reactive, these are the first lessons that your new puppy will likely learn. If she is coping with stress by barking, lunging and aggressing, chances are higher the puppies will also engage in this behavior as they get older. It doesn't matter how cute your puppy is—you might have to say no to the breeder and pick another avenue of obtaining a puppy.

Pertaining to health, respected breeders have their puppies all cleared by a veterinarian, and the dogs on the premises all look healthy. When the puppy goes home, a vaccine and health history will be sent with the dog, as well as information on food, the personality of the puppy, and considerations that need to be made for that specific dog. They will not let a puppy go before the recommended eight-twelve weeks of age (recommendations made by both the AKC and top behavior specialists). Prior to eight weeks of age, the puppy is losing out on critical learning from mom and the litter. Adoption before that time is not recommended by trainers, behavior specialists and reputable breeders, as a means to head off potential physical and behavior problems down the line.

Owners Mariah and Alan Torpey of Somerville, Massachusetts looked far and wide for a breed that suited their lifestyle. They know that playing for a few hours a day with Roger the Aussie is mandatory...and that's ok for them!

Make sure you do your research and find breeders who breed for personality and companionship instead of for more intense jobs, if you are looking for a purebred companion in the city. There are breeding lines of golden retrievers that are bred specifically to be social, and breeding lines of golden retrievers bred specifically to engage in hunting. Both will need aerobic exercise and training, but one will be more satisfied with a romp in a park chasing a ball, while the other will likely require miles of hiking, specialized sports training, and more work on the part of the owner to be happy in the city. If you want a Rhodesian ridgeback in the city as a running buddy (an excellent choice for distance runners), you want one bred for personality, not necessarily a dog selected for intense hunting trials. There aren't a lot of lions running around Boston, so if you have a high prey-drive ridgeback, you are likely going to have a difficult time managing your 80 pound lion hunter on runs through pigeon-infested Copley Square. Personality really does matter, so look for breeders who feel the same way. When you meet the puppy, take note of the following:

- What are the parents like?
- Are the puppies playful and active?
- Are they shy, shaking and quivering in the corner?
- Is the puppy interested in toys, food, or affection?

These are all clues to the personality of your puppy, which can be shaped, but not totally altered. An extroverted dog will have a hard time being an introvert, so be cognizant of what it is that you are selecting.

Conversely, most puppies will eventually come out of their shell, but that doesn't mean an introverted puppy will love being in a boisterous environment.

Recent studies by the aptly named Clever Dog Lab in Vienna (part of the **Messerli Research Institute) state** that formal puppy temperament tests do not adequately predict an adult dog's behavior[3]. Some experts swear by formal tests of one kind or another, while other experts scoff at the idea. For starters, breeds and tests vary greatly, and these tests are very subjective. I can interpret something one way, and my breeder can interpret it a different way. These tests are helpful in the same way that horoscopes and Rorschach tests are helpful: you see what you want to see, and maybe that can be useful going forward. It's not the only indicator of success. Genetics matter. Environment matters. Rearing matters a great deal. If a puppy is aggressing or fearful at eight weeks old more so than the rest of the litter, I would personally take that into consideration. If I were going to a breeder, I'd likely be looking more closely at the adult dogs on the premises to see how they are doing, as a means of figuring out the personality of my soon-to-be-pup.

Thousands of puppies are sold every day. Not every puppy sold is from a reputable breeder. That said, many of these puppies do turn out to be fantastic dogs. I had a roommate who had an amazing pup who was ordered and shipped online. There was a lot of luck, and I'm sure the breeder really loved his puppies, but what if my roommate didn't end up with a happy puppy, or if the puppy got sick in the first week? There wouldn't have been a whole lot he could have done.

In short, it's on you to do your homework, and it's on the breeders to do theirs. As long as everyone is above board, you are giving yourself the best possible chance of finding a suitable match. It might take a lot longer to get the right dog, but after seeing what can happen when shortcuts are taken, I can tell you, it's worth taking the time to do it right. If your breeder answers all of your questions, you've developed a good mutual rapport, and you found the breed you feel will fit your lifestyle the best, absolutely get a dog from a *well-researched* breeder who will let you handle the puppies, meet the mom, and work with you to make the best possible decision. As you'll see in the next chapter, always, always put your hands on the dogs first—regardless of your decision to get a purebred puppy from a reputable breeder, or from a reliable rescue organization.

---

[3] Riemer S, Müller C, Virányi Z, Huber L, Range F (2014) *The Predictive Value of Early Behavioural Assessments in Pet Dogs – A Longitudinal Study from Neonates to Adults.* PLoS ONE 9(7): e101237. doi:10.1371/journal.pone.0101237

Shelters and Rescues

How to rescue, responsibly

Finding a Reputable Shelter or Rescue: Not All Shelters Are Equal

When you go to a shelter, it's quite an emotional experience. The sounds, the sad little faces, the cages—it's one of the hardest places to walk into. All of these dogs have a story to tell. They are there for a variety of reasons, including:

- Behavior issues
- Family didn't have enough time for the dog
- Pulled from a hoarding situation
- Criminal Cases
- Abandoned
- Stray
- Family moved and couldn't take the dog
- Military owner had to leave the dog behind

Our shelters are overrun, the volunteers and staff are overworked, and there doesn't seem to be an end in sight. Many potential owners make the decision to adopt a dog from a shelter or pound, which saves a life. In Massachusetts, we have a higher ratio of "no-kill" shelters than many other states, but that's a misnomer. These shelters will humanely euthanize dogs that are too sick or too aggressive to re-home safely. These dogs are suffering and it's kinder to let these dogs go humanely and with dignity. Contrast that with high-kill shelters that are so full that the only option to make room for the dogs that are coming in is to euthanize the dogs that have been in the shelter the longest.

People who want a purebred dog and also want to rescue are able to satisfy both desires by going through a breed-specific rescue agency. If you can find a reputable shelter or rescue, then the dogs undergo a thorough behavior evaluation, temperament exam, and a physical exam to ensure that the dog is placed correctly. Not all purebred dogs end up in breed-specific rescue, and not all breed-specific rescues are perfect, but if you have your heart set on a purebred dog and want to rescue, there is a way to do both. When working with a breed-specific rescue, make sure that you are following the same protocol as you would when searching for a reputable shelter.

Ajax in Cincinnati.
He is loved by Chris and Flannery Geier of Somerville, Massachusetts

According to the Humane Society of the United States, 25% of all dogs in shelters are purebred. These are dogs whose owners wanted a particular type of dog, but ended up in over their heads, because they didn't do their homework. These are puppies from online breeders who sold the puppy without doing proper evaluations of the family first. These are dogs that were poorly bred or sick, and the new owners couldn't afford care. These are puppies that were shipped without having met the family first, so when things didn't work out there was no contingency plan in place. These are puppies that were sold as part of a puppy mill operation to owners who really didn't know what type of business they were supporting. These are all dogs that have one thing in common: if the owners had met the breeder and the dogs first, different decisions might have been made, and our shelters would house a lot fewer dogs.

This Great Pyrenees is a purebred dog. She was photographed by Melissa Mullen of Melissa Mullen Photography. Many pro-photographers, like Melissa, volunteer at shelters like the Animal Welfare Society in Kennebunk, Maine. It's hard to walk in and leave the dogs behind, but photographers volunteer their time to help get shelter dogs, like this purebred Pyrenees, a permanent home.

According to *The Boston Globe*[4], approximately 14,000 dogs were trucked in and rescued legally through Massachusetts rescue agencies in 2012. Many of these dogs do really well in any environment, but some of these dogs might only do well with a quiet family without a lot of visitors, in a quiet neighborhood, and not a lot of change to the environment. Puppies and dogs that are shut down and scared will do less-well in cities like Boston, living in an apartment complex, with doors constantly opening, closing, neighbors coming and going, or upstairs neighbors chasing their (loud) toddler. The dogs that are more sensitive to sound might not cope as well with garbage trucks, skateboards, traffic, or other loud noises that are part of the hustle and bustle of the city. You won't know this until you see the dog in a city environment.

The veterinarians in our region are seeing medical issues in our rescued dogs, too. They are reporting more diseases, like Rocky Mountain

[4] Kim Kavin, "The Good, the Bad and the Biters," *The Boston Globe,* May 12, 2013 http://www.bostonglobe.com/magazine/2013/05/11/regulating-dog-rescues-massachusetts/g0GHFp1M81WcAZhqhURoOO/story.html

spotted fever, parvovirus, and others that previously were uncommon in the Commonwealth. This is because of the high numbers of dogs being trucked into our shelters and rescues from other parts of the country without first being properly tested for diseases (This also includes puppy mills that ship sick dogs to unsuspecting families). NPR's *Morning Edition*[5] ran a story on how dogs flown in from India, Puerto Rico, Iraq and Thailand have come into the country with rabies. One family in Vermont had to euthanize their newly adopted dog after it developed the disease.

Meanwhile, dogs that come into the shelter locally tend to get overlooked. Perhaps they aren't as "exotic" or interesting. What started off saving dogs from places less fortunate has become, to some degree (conscious or not) a marketing technique that works to move dogs, but something is wickedly broken.

A trained raccoon hunter in rural Tennessee might not be the best candidate for an urban environment. While that might seem obvious, there is one down the street from my home who is working with a friend of mine, a certified behavior specialist. This particular dog is really freaked out, especially on trash day. This is a dog that was placed from a rescue agency in our area that places thousands of dogs annually in urban environments. Sadly, when I see the name of this group on my evaluations, I already know what's coming. In this particular case, which is not an uncommon occurrence in the Metro-Boston area, she was placed completely out of her element. The humane thing in this case would be to have the owner bring her back to the shelter, or spend thousands of dollars on behavior specialists and hope everything pans out. This is a dog that has a lot to overcome, and now the owners have to spend the rest of this dog's life helping her cope medically and emotionally. What this family wanted was a dog to take to the park and have a buddy, and what they got was a sweet dog that is living her life as a ball of stress. Had the coonhound been evaluated and placed correctly by the agency that had her, or the new owners thought through what having an outdoor hunting dog in a densely populated city would be like, she might have been placed somewhere more suitable, and this topic would never have come up.

Keep in mind that everyone's Modus Operandi was to save this dog—the shelter in Tennessee that shipped her; the rescue group in Massachusetts that placed her; the family who took her.

Let me be perfectly clear: A dog isn't saved just because it's no longer

---

[5] Morning Edition, *With Rescue Dogs in Demand, More Shelters Look Far Afield for Fido*, January 1, 2015: http://www.wbur.org/npr/374257591/with-rescue-dogs-in-demand-more-shelters-look-far-afield-for-fido.

in a shelter. A dog needs to thrive physically and emotionally to be truly rescued. Owners need to be honest about what they can handle, but rescue groups need to be forthcoming about the clinically under-socialized dogs they are sending into our urban centers.

What to look for in a good rescue organization:

In defense of rescue groups, many are working so hard to keep afloat and get enough food for the dogs, that they don't have time to evaluate the dog for you, or have the proper training to conduct evaluations. Many groups are run by volunteers who are really trying to help. Some groups are unaware that there are resources available to help with behavior assessment, like the Match-Up II, the Humane Society of the United States website, and Kelly Dunbar's Open Paw program, to name a few.

A behavior evaluation from a reputable shelter can provide the best chance of finding just the right personality of dog for your family and environment, or at least provide information regarding what issues the dog has while providing a supportive staff to assist with those potential issues. I've seen many owners try to find help through the shelter for aggression, fear, or a mismatch issue post-adoption only to be ignored. In some less-reputable shelters and rescue groups, dogs are just numbers. They were "saved" so they have to make room for the next dog; it's simply no longer their problem. They might not have the staffing or expertise to deal with all the complications post-adoption.

A good shelter or rescue agency will answer your call and have classes run by certified trainers. Some even have behavior specialists on staff. If they don't have these things, they should at least have a list of reputable resources available to you so you don't feel utterly stuck. They want to make sure that each dog has found a forever home, and they will do what they can to make sure everything is copacetic. If you can find a shelter that conducts a thorough behavior exam, like the Match-Up II evaluation conducted through the Animal Rescue League of Boston, you are starting off on the right foot.

If your only option is to adopt from a group who can't do the recommended temperament exams, bring a certified trainer or consultant with you. Some certified professional dog trainers (CPDT) offer this as part of their training packages. Talk with someone who is qualified to help you find the right pet for your situation prior to visiting the shelter.

Additionally, some dogs are too stressed in shelters to pass a temperament test in-house. A good behavior evaluator can usually determine if a dog would do better off-site. Make sure you are making a wise decision, not purely an emotional one, which is incredibly hard to do when you are in a shelter environment and those sad little eyes are staring right up at you.

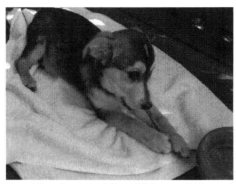

Maura Kennedy and Steve Turcott rescued "Bandit" from a shelter outside of Boston. Bandit had an unknown history but now that doesn't even matter. He loves mechanical reindeer, barking at dogs, agility, naps and Bully sticks.

Lastly, if you choose to get a dog for the city, I generally recommend looking at urban shelters. There are thousands of dogs in the suburbs and rural areas that do need help. These shelters are able house more animals, but if you live in the city, it's best to see how your potential dog does on a walk in the city. How does the dog cope with city noises and people? How did the dog respond to a truck that drove by? You won't get to find these things out if you get a dog in a rural shelter, until after you bring it home to live in your condo on Main Street.

I can make the same argument for online rescue sites. Just like with breeders, I always suggest putting your hands on the dog first and taking it for a test-run, for obvious reasons. I have been running a non-scientific experiment with a popular homeless-pet search database. Each week, I pop on to search for dogs within 100 miles of my home outside of Boston. The first three pages are dogs in Houston, Alabama, Louisiana and other places that will ship a dog to me. I'm not a geography buff, but I'm pretty sure Texas is more than a two-hour drive from Boston. Some groups use bogus shelter names or falsify a location to get under the radar. Just like with breeding operations, if you cannot put your hands on the dog, no matter how cute it is, my advice is to pass and go to a shelter, so you can see the dogs first hand. (I have alerted this website to this phenomenon in the hopes to make their search algorithm better, like adding a search function for dogs that are physically in a searchable location or making sure they have a foster family in the area first. They stated that they can't fix this issue at this time, so it's on you to really make sure that the rescue group is in driving distance).

I can't stress enough how important it is to go and see the dog first hand. If you feel strongly about a particular dog, then get on a plane. Go see the dog and fly back with it. It's better to know in person if this isn't a match than to find out when the dog is in an airport and you are in over your head.

I see dogs after they are homed, and there are great rescue groups that I never get the opportunity to work with because they do a great job matching dogs to people. They have resources available to owners. Some examples in Massachusetts include the MSPCA, the Animal Rescue League of Boston, Save-a-Dog, and the smaller Scituate Animal Shelter. These facilities have programs to make sure these dogs are successfully homed the first time in the city, and if not, they make sure they help the owners and the dogs in whatever way they can without leaving them stranded. Make sure the group you are working with in your state is reputable.

Rescues By Truck: Are You Saving A Dog?

In the Northeast, dogs are frequently trucked in from the South and the Midwest, where the ratio of kill shelters is higher: up to 90% of dogs in some southern shelters are euthanized according to Kavin's *The Good, the Bad and the Biters*. Every year, 14,000 of these dogs are brought legally into the Commonwealth to find loving homes, where they wouldn't otherwise have a chance. This seems wonderful on paper. There are a lot of dogs that would otherwise be euthanized and by bringing these dogs north, there's a better chance of finding them a forever home. Thousands of dogs brought in this way have been amazing pets to their new owners over the years, but many dogs that are trucked in are often not evaluated behaviorally or physically prior to being transported to their new home.

Massachusetts, in response to spikes of behavior issues, and a rise of highly contagious illnesses from the dogs being shipped up via doggie under-hound railroad, enacted an emergency law in 2005:

"...all dogs coming into the state for rescue must remain quarantined until proven behaviorally and physically sound for adoption."

To get around these laws, because with every law there is a loophole, truckloads of dogs and puppies meet potential owners just over the border in Connecticut, Rhode Island and New Hampshire, where owners are handed the puppy they were promised. Some internet rescue sites will ship dogs to owners with the promise that you never have to meet the dog first. "We'll match it to you. Just take our word for it! It's a great dog and will love you unconditionally." If you read the chapter on how to find a reliable breeder, this should sound remarkably similar to the groups you should not work with.

This speaks well for the rescue agency's numbers. They are easily able to move and "save" as many dogs as they possibly can, but the matching process is insufficient. The rescue agency needs to turn over dogs, so they can keep up with the numbers of homeless pets. They are driven to save the dogs, but sometimes they're saving dogs by placing them with people in environments that are not suited for that animal. There is a minimal matching process in many of these programs. All the while truckloads of sick dogs are coming into the state, there is no vet care during transport (and sometimes, prior to transport), and there are no behavior evaluations conducted at any point. In many cases, the first sign that something is amiss is when a dog trainer or behavior consultant is called into a home, weeks after the adoption when the dog is growling, barking, noise reactive, submissively peeing when people enter the home, or biting family members.

Imagine you are a puppy in Tennessee, and had spent the first three months of your life in the wild. Then an Animal Control Officer finds you and puts you on a truck in which you are shipped with several dozen other terrified puppies and dogs. After driving 1,000 miles to a rest stop in Connecticut, you are taken out, separated from your family, and given to people, that you may, or may not, be ok with. You drive off in a Honda Civic to your new home in Cambridge, Massachusetts—an urban environment with dump trucks, thousands of dogs, and people in every direction. That is the extent of many of these "matching" programs from rescue groups that truck dogs out of danger. "Do you have a credit card? You are matched!"

Some of these dogs can be wonderful companions, and many do extraordinarily well living in a northern metropolis with a little training and the right equipment, but equally as many of these dogs are anxious, shut down, and under-socialized. They might have been totally fine had they not been shipped under these incredibly stressful conditions, or if they were able to acclimate in a foster home prior to living with a family.

Many of these dogs descend from highly specialized animals bred for hunting, tracking, and working, which are then released to the wild when they no longer perform to the standards of the owner. These high prey-drive dogs then shack up in the woods (as dogs tend to do!) where they have a litter of genetically high prey-drive puppies. Most of these puppies don't interact with people until they are trapped and trucked to the North, all in the name of saving them.

When a dog's first experience with people is from the inside of a humane trap, and that dog is loaded onto a truck where there are other scared dogs, significant issues can arise. The dogs ride in this truck, often for a two to three day journey, or longer. They travel in a crate, which is the safest way to transport these dogs. Crates can be a useful house-training tool when used correctly, but when a dog's first experience with one is on a truck for a long journey, it can make house-training and confining a challenge. Keeping a dog confined with other barking, frightened dogs for a multi-day journey can absolutely have a long term effect on a dog's relationship to vehicles, other dogs, and strangers. Trauma at any point may lead to behavioral breakdowns, weeks, months or even years later.

If a rescue group can't legally function in the borders of a state, but is willing to transport outside of those state lines, that is a group that is not willing to do things above board. These groups are harming the behavioral and physical welfare of the dogs they work with, and are putting the families who adopt these dogs at great risk. They are intentionally looking for loopholes to boost their numbers and move as many dogs as possible. On paper, these groups are saving thousands of dogs a year, and that is a fantastic calling. These rescue groups are mostly volunteers who give up their weekends, time with their family to save dogs, and that is noble. However, because proper evaluations aren't made and proper considerations aren't made for the eventual behavioral welfare of these dogs long-term, many end up in mismatched situations. These dogs are later re-homed, drugged, or euthanized after living their entire lives completely overwhelmed and stressed out. There is a much better way to save our dogs.

One of my recent students rescued a dog over the Massachusetts border in Rhode Island. When she picked up her dog, he was very sick and required immediate medical attention. She happened to be a veterinary student at Tufts, so she recognized the signs of medical distress sooner than someone not trained in the medical field, and the puppy was able to get appropriate care. According to this owner, of the dogs that came up on that truck, half of them died and the other half needed significant medical attention. Remember that these dogs were promoted as "healthy, happy puppies". If they were legally brought into the state, they would have had to go through a quarantine period to ensure their health status and to make sure they would not pass diseases to other dogs in the neighborhood. I would say that if these dogs were cared for before the road trip, some might have been euthanized prior to the journey, but the rest of the dogs might not have fallen ill, and some who passed away might have survived. I saw this student's dog for behavior issues related to his reactions to a highly stimulating city environment after a year of being with his owners. This is the same story I hear over and over again in my region.

Never, NEVER take a dog home that you meet off a truck at a highway rest stop. Similarly, **NEVER take a dog home that you haven't met first. This rule is applicable for breeders, shelters, and rescue agencies.**

There are literally hundreds of dogs in your area that need a home. Some of these dogs were trucked in from other places, but at least you can meet the dogs first without the pressure of standing on I-95 with a truck full of dogs that NEED YOU NOW. Putting dogs through the stress of traveling by plane, truck, or other means of transport to meet you at a roadside rest stop before going home is not an ideal way to start things off. It's impossible to evaluate if a dog in a Citgo parking lot can thrive in a highly stimulating city environment. That dog is in shock, and the people are excited for their new puppy that they just saved. Emotions are high from all parties. Too many of these dogs are saved, only to find themselves in an environment so anxiety provoking that they need medication and management for the rest of their lives.

There are great fostering groups who will pick dogs up from trucks in parking lots and highway rest stops. These are trained volunteers who take these dogs, evaluate them, get the appropriate vet care they require, and then pair owners up, once more is known about a particular dog. For a potential dog owner who has never had experience with a truck full of dogs that are "matched" specifically, it's incredibly overwhelming. Leave it to the pros, and wait for a dog you meet, face to face. I don't mean that you wait in a parking lot for three minutes before you take the dog home. I mean that you should wait for the right group and work with that group, or go to a shelter where you can take a dog out for a walk and see if there is a potential for a lifelong bond.

Breeder or Rescue: Common Ground for the Potential Owner

It's worth it to take a few weeks, or months, to research the dogs that will do well with your family *and your environment.* This will lessen the risk of having to manage a behavior-related problem due to overstimulation, and lessen the likelihood of being mismatched from the get-go. It's not fair to the dog to be drugged if it was better off in the country. It's not fair to the family who wanted a bomb-proof, happy dog to play with their kids and take on trips, if the dog can't handle children or changes of scenery. Find the rescues and breeders who have a good track record of doing the right thing.

- Regardless of shelter, rescue or breeding facilities, do check with the Better Business Bureau first to make sure that there are no complaints on file.

- Don't ship a dog unless you have previously put your hands on the dog. Even if the dog or puppy is from a breeder or a rescue group, it's imperative to see the pet first. The best matching programs can be wrong. Match.com might make a great match on paper, but I personally wouldn't sign a pre-nup without meeting the other person first. Chemistry goes a long way, and the same is true for dog ownership.

- Pay attention to the other dogs. It's easy to get laser focused on "that dog" or "that puppy," but what do the other dogs look like? Is everyone healthy? If not, are the sick dogs quarantined?

- Some dogs need behavior modification medication for legitimate reasons, and that will be addressed later in the book; however, the numbers of dogs going on these drugs just so they can cope is going through the roof, as a direct result of poor breeding, poor placement, owners not being honest about the type of dog that suits them, rescues and breeders not being honest about the type of dog they are selling, and dogs coming off trucks at rest stops moving into the city. Some are seriously under-socialized to people and urban environments. If more dogs were paired correctly from the beginning, I would wager that fewer cases would require behavior modification medication.

- Talk with certified trainers or behavior specialists in your area to see if they can recommend a shelter, breeder, or rescue group that does a good job pairing people to dogs. Not all shelters and rescues are on the up and up; not all breeders are breeding for family life. (To put things in perspective, there are hundreds of rescues and shelters around Boston. I only recommend four of them. The same goes for Labrador breeders in my region).

- Always meet the dog first to make sure it's a good match for you and your family before taking the dog home.

- If you feel pressured at all by the rescue group or the breeder, don't do it, no matter how cute the dog is. It's worth taking the time to do your homework to avoid additional expenditures, medications and heartache.

- You can still help the dog if things don't feel right. Call the local animal control officer if you suspect there is inhumane treatment, a puppy mill operation, a rescue that isn't above board, neglect, or other serious offenses. If animal control can't help, call the Humane Society or ASPCA. They will be able to work with the proper authorities to get the dogs the help they need. The rule of thumb on train systems, airports and the dog industry is the same: If you see something, say something.

A well-vetted dog that is satisfied mentally, gets enough exercise, gets plenty of attention from the owners, and gets regular training and vet visits can thrive in a city environment, but you have to do your homework first. Dogs in the city need to have structure and feel safe in a loud environment built for people. Cities are our home, and dogs are invited to live here, too, but not all dogs are city dogs. That's totally ok, but as people, we need to be honest about that, and stop dragging dogs that are not suited for city life into our urban centers.

I know that this is a tough chapter. In the following chapters are success stories of dogs in the city. Some are rescues, and some are from highly regarded breeders. If you do your homework, know what to look for, and can find reputable resources to support you along the way, you and your new dog will have the best shot at a good first step on this long walk together.

Michelle Winer says this of her best friend, Eva:
She is the happiest dog on the planet, one who was thrown away like trash and came very
close to being put down in a kill shelter in Tennessee. As you can see she clearly is not trash,
she's a love bug who loves attention, snuggles and popcorn.
She now lives like a queen.

If we could all be as happy as Eva, the world would certainly be a better place!

Entourage

All the people to add to your holiday card list!

Dogs in highly populated cities tend to have entourages in addition to their families. There are veterinarians, health specialists, day care providers, dog-walkers, trainers, and boarding facilities for dogs that can't travel with their owners, to name just a few people your dog will likely have on staff. There are trusted resources in most communities, but you have to know where to look, and know what you're looking for.

Box Stores:

The big chain stores are really convenient, and it's often the first place to hit after getting a new canine companion. They have everything you need all in one location! It's almost a rite of passage once you get your dog. It's important to note that though they have everything, including dog training, daycares, veterinarians, and groomers at these facilities, the services tend not to be as great as you would get from a local trainer who is certified, or a veterinarian who works at a stand-alone hospital. Though there are great service providers who work at the box stores, you'll do better going to a facility specializing in individual services.

Instead, go to the box stores for supplies, food, and special treats. Better yet, go to a locally owned pet boutique—but leave the services to the professionals who have been working at a facility designed for training, grooming or medical care. I wouldn't go to Kmart for a haircut, and I wouldn't go to a box store for a specialized service.

Django at Pet Spa, a locally owned grooming salon in Somerville, MA.
No cages here! It's party time, all the time, for dogs that can handle this environment.
Owned by Phyllis Ewen

Trainers:

This is my specialty, so it's only appropriate to start here. A dog trainer is the person you ask for training and behavior advice in the same way you ask a veterinarian about health, vaccines and that weird rash on your dog's nose. The field has come a long way from where it was even a decade ago. Science, research, YouTube, certifications and television have all increased the awareness of what dog training can do, and have eliminated the taboo that only difficult dogs go to class. The downside is, until recently, anyone who has ever owned, walked, or looked at a dog, could put a sign up in their window declaring they were a dog trainer. The challenge was determining who was qualified, who was good, and who was going to work well for a particular issue.

Certifications now exist in order to help separate the wheat from the chaff. There is more on this in later chapters, but look for a trainer who is certified in dog training, and has taken a test in learning theory. For example, the test I took, and passed, was up to four hours in length. It covered a variety of subjects, including animal husbandry, learning theory, teaching methods, equipment, ethics and ethology. I had to prove I was an effective lead trainer for over 300 hours by collecting statements from previous students, other teachers in the field, and get the approval of my techniques from a veterinarian. There are other certifications that are harder, others that are easier, but it's important to note that people who are willing to improve their skill set and take an exam proving that they know their science, as well as their art, are probably willing to stay above board in training techniques and ethics. There are exceptions, but generally this is a good starting point.

Make sure that your instructor is personable with people. It's not enough to love dogs, or to be an excellent handler. They need to effectively communicate what they are doing with a dog to a human being. Someone who doesn't love working with both species is not someone you should have in your corner.

If trainers have your best interest at heart, they won't be advocating for the use of harsh, outdated equipment like prong collars, shock collars, and choke chains. The science on these devices has proven again, and again, and again that there is much more harm physically than initially thought. If these tools aren't used correctly, dogs can behaviorally unwind, leading to more significant behavior problems like aggression towards people and dogs, or fearful behavior.

Bulldog puppy, Oscar, wasn't into playing fetch. In fact, he was pretty terrible at it.

Oscar's owner employed Janet Vera, owner of For the Love of Dogs, to find what he liked to do. If you want a skateboarding bulldog, a trainer specializing in positive reinforcement techniques can help! The key is to find something your pet likes to do and work with that skill.

The University of Lincoln, in London, recently published a study stating that even when used according to the manufacturer of shock collars, dogs that were trained by shocks showed mannerisms consistent with an increase in stress when compared to two different control groups[6]. In my experience, an increase in stress leads to a shorter fuse and an increase in significant behaviors that need immediate attention. There are better tools and equipment to help teach a dog to walk, and better equipment available to help you teach your dog to behave. Look for a trainer who advocates for the use of those kinder, more effective tools that work with you to *train* behaviors that you prefer, not just suppress behaviors with a snazzy tool. The more a behavior is suppressed with a device, the more likely that device will fail in time.

You will never see a reputable trainer or teacher use an "alpha roll," which is a technique in which the dog is pinned to the ground on his back as a way to make him "submit." Additionally, reputable trainers will not talk about dominance theory as a means of effectively training a dog, or use phrases like "the wolves do it this way, so does your dog." We are no more chimps than these dogs are wolves. The best writer on this subject is John Bradshaw, in case you have an itch to scratch on the subject. In his book *Dog Sense*, he not only debunks the long-held theory that dogs need an alpha because wolves have an alpha, but illustrates perfectly that we don't even understand wolf behavior as we once did, back when dominance theory was really at its peak.

Dogs have been domesticated over thousands of years, unlike our wolf friends who are very much wild animals that have their own complex social structures. A goofy pug has the same chance of survival and acceptance in a wolf pack as I do in a chimpanzee community. Zero. We need to stop treating our dogs as wolves, because they aren't. They are dogs.

In the event you need a little more persuasion on the matter, submission in a wolf pack is *earned*, never forced, unlike the alpha rolling techniques that are highlighted on certain television shows about dog training. That alone should be the nail in the coffin for dominance theory. If a dog is growling, lunging and barking at a stimulus, a reputable dog trainer will never "put him in his place." Instead, a good trainer will effectively teach the dog what you want by paying close attention to the dog's body language, and hopefully never allow the dog to feel so stressed out that it will react in an aggressive or fearful manner. Confidence and accomplishments are built over time.

Reputable trainers will never say they are something they're not, or that

---

[6] Cooper JJ, Cracknell N, Hardiman J, Wright H, Mills D (2014) *The Welfare Consequences and Efficacy of Training Pet Dogs with Remote Electronic Training Collars in Comparison to Reward Based Training*, PLoS ONE 9(9): e102722. doi:10.1371/journal.pone.0102722

they "specialize" in particular breeds of dogs. I love Border collies and herding dogs, but the only way I specialize in them is when I'm teaching sports that tend to attract the owners of these dogs. I also would warn that if a trainer suggests they won't work with a particular breed of dog, then they're likely someone who isn't going to work very well for any kind of dog.

Lastly, a good trainer will know when to back out and let a more specialized professional take over. There is an entire chapter dedicated to these related professions (trainers, consultants and behaviorists), what each does, and how to find the right professional for you.

Veterinarians:

It's not always easy to figure out where to take a sick pet when something unexpected happens, as it undoubtedly will. Your vet has heard everything from, "My dog is limping and I don't know why," to "My Boxer swallowed my briefs." We need to know our vets are qualified at what they do, and also that they enjoy the job.

There are many specialties in the veterinary field. Are you interested in holistic treatments? There are vets who specialize in or supplement their care with homeopathic treatments. Do you prefer a big teaching hospital where you might not see the same vet twice but they are always able to see to your pet's needs, or would you prefer a smaller practice, where you get personalized care and attention from the same vet over a lifetime? Is there an emergency hospital nearby? This is hopefully the beginning of a lifelong relationship, so it's important to choose carefully and know what's available.

If you have a friend with a dog, you can start by asking who their veterinarian is, and if they feel comfortable with their services. You can try Yelp or Angie's List to get a good feel about what people are saying, but keep in mind that one negative review should not be weighted heavier than twenty exemplary ones. That said, if all of the reviews are terrible, you might want to look for a different provider for your pet's care. If most of the dogs in your neighborhood are going to a particular vet in your area (or, perhaps to a vet just outside of your area) it's probably a good sign that this is a vet that you should also get on board with.

"Kaiju," a Shiba inu, suffered an injury as a puppy. He needed physical therapy, so his bones and muscles could grow correctly. His owner, Nobuko Ichikawa took this photo of him on a surfboard during his session at FlowDog in Waltham, Massachusetts.

After you've checked the reviews, narrow your field down to two or three clinics. It's recommended that you look at the websites of local clinics, and ask the hospital manager for a tour, so you can meet some of the staff, see the rooms, the surgery area, and all of the areas your pet will likely be spending some time in at one point or another. Additionally, check the Office of Consumer Affairs and Business Regulation to make sure that there have been no serious issues that have been reported. Each state has its own office. Here is the one for Massachusetts: http://www.mass.gov/ocabr/licensee/dpl-boards/vt/. All of this will help you make the best possible decision for your pet's health.

Good bedside manner is an invaluable skill that not all veterinarians have. These are the professionals who love what they do, are good with dogs, cats, (birds, horses and guinea pigs if they are into that sort of thing!), as well as people. You need to feel you can tell your vet anything, no matter how weird, and they can handle it. My vets have a lovely sense of humor, but they also know when to be extra sensitive when bad news is delivered. That's a hard line to walk, and they do it with dignity and experience. If you find these veterinarians, tell everyone about them so they can continue to give excellent care to as many pets as possible. If those vets are not seeing additional clients, ask for their recommendation so you can make certain that you are getting similar, reliable care for your pet. If you move, ask if they can recommend someone in your new area.

The chances are good that they know someone, or can help you find excellent care.

Daycare Providers and Dog-Walking Services:

Our dogs give up a lot to live with us in the city. They rarely get to freely roam or go for long walks in the woods every single day. The ones who do have these opportunities are very lucky. Instead, our dogs tend to live in an apartment building with doors that slam shut, or paper-thin walls where you can hear everything from the neighbors next door.

Your pup might watch other dogs walking down the street, see kids playing, or hear the bustle of traffic outside of his window, while he is stuck inside all day long. Sure, you left him a bone to chew, but that doesn't occupy most dogs for an entire day. Most working adults are gone for eight to ten hours at a time, which is a long period for a dog to be left alone with nothing to do but pine.

Consider for a moment purebred dogs like Border collies who are bred to run over mountains up to ten miles a day (the sheep go ten miles—the dogs are going upwards of one-hundred miles daily, circling the sheep), or mastiffs who are bred to protect property. These dogs are looking out the window all day long, stressing about the dozens of pedestrians on *their* street. This is also incredibly hard for puppies that need to get out to pee every couple of hours and explore their surroundings, like all young mammals need to do. A cookie when you walk out the front door is just not going to cut it.

With more people choosing specific dog breeds that have high energy capacities, and higher energy dogs rescued from secluded areas, people are now realizing that all dogs need much more mental and physical exercise to be happier in the city. It was inevitable that daycares, dog-walkers and other service providers would start to pop up, but how do you pick the service that is right for your dog?

Is My Dog A Candidate For Daycare?

Daycare is expensive but it's a fantastic resource for high-energy dogs that like to play, run, and engage with other dogs. It's also great for dogs that need more supervision. In the Boston area, a full day in a non box-store daycare runs anywhere from $30-40 daily for six+ hours. There are hourly and half day options available as well. Many even offer additional services for pickup and drop off, so your dog gets door-to-door service from a personal chauffeur. If you can afford daycare, this might be a good option, even if it's only once a week.

Mighty Moose the Pug is in there somewhere!
Photo by his dedicated owner, Kim Tran

Daycare is appropriate for:
- Dogs that genuinely love to play with other dogs.
- Dogs that have higher energy requirements.
- Dogs that might be destructive if left alone all day, or suffer from boredom.
- Some dogs that suffer from separation anxiety, but not all cases. Consult with a specialist.
- Owners who feel bad about leaving their dog alone all day, provided the dog also likes other dogs, and fits in well in a daycare environment.

Daycare is NOT appropriate for:
- Dogs that get anxious around toys or resource guard (these dogs might growl, snap, or be otherwise uncomfortable with people and dogs near their food, toys, and other resources).
- Dogs that are nervous, reactive or aggressive around other dogs.
- Dogs that don't cope well with a changing environment.
- Dogs that prefer to sleep all day.
- Dogs that have medical issues, such as arthritis, because rambunctious puppies jumping on sore joints can lead to a bad

experience for everyone involved.

- Dogs that we affectionately call "The Fun Police." These are dogs that bark and try to break up dogs that are otherwise having a good time.
- Dogs that don't read body language cues or are socially awkward. These dogs would also do better with alternative arrangements. These dogs might seem like bullies or pushy, like the kids on the playground who might wrestle just a little too hard, or be a little too competitive, not realizing they are hurting their play-pal.

When selecting a daycare:
- Make sure the staff is knowledgeable and friendly.
- Your dog is required to pass a behavior examination before being admitted to a daycare session.
- Make sure you are required to sign appropriate waivers.
- Consider what is included in the behavior evaluation, and consider if you feel comfortable that all the dogs in the space passed the evaluation (the more stringent, the better it is for your dog).
- Do you feel comfortable walking into the facility? Do you feel your dog is cared for, and that other dogs are being carefully selected?
- Ask where the dogs relieve themselves—in cities, space is a commodity. I've seen daycares where dogs are either expected to "hold it" all day, or are expected to pee on the floors (hello, regression in house-training). Make sure the dogs are either walked, or have a space on the property where they can do their business.

You also should be asked for a vaccination history, including proof of rabies, distemper, and in most facilities, kennel cough (also known as *bordetella*). The facility should be clean, and dogs should be happy. If the place smells like urine, fecal matter, or is just really dirty, then you should consider other options for your dog. If any of the dogs look unhealthy or are behaviorally unsound, pick another facility to care for your pet.

Make sure the business is fully insured to have dogs, and that the play space can accommodate the number of dogs in the play space adequately. Overcrowding can be a problem, so you want to make sure that the dogs have plenty of room to run and tumble! There should also be a separate space for smaller dogs, or for dogs to have a break if they need it. Also consider that puppies might need a place to sleep, or be fed, and that should be a solitary area where they can really have some space.

If the play supervisor won't let you watch play, you may wish to consider a new facility, but it shouldn't be the sole reason to nix a daycare. Many dogs get over excited when they see their owners, which can pose an issue for daycare providers and the safety of the dogs in the play space; however, many facilities have a window that you can look through, or an area for observation where you can take a peek to make sure your dog is having a good time. One facility in our area uses closed circuit TV so owners can watch from a different room, while the play supervisor and the dogs act as they normally would in the play space. This ensures that the dogs don't get too jazzed up, which keeps everyone safe.

Dog-Walkers/Playgroups

Dog-walkers in the city are a cost-effective way of making sure urban hounds get out for a walk at least once per day. There are many services a dog-walking provider might offer, including playgroups at a local dog park, hiking with a group, group walks in the neighborhood, or solo walks.

Dogs enjoying a mid-day romp at Nunziato Dog Park in Somerville, MA
Photo by Pat Dains, OnTheRunBoston.com

Playgroups or Group Walks:
Dogs that go on group outings get the benefit of playing and interacting with other dogs while also sniffing, stretching their legs and engaging with

a trusted person for 20-60 minutes (typically) per outing. This tends to be the most cost-effective way of meeting your dog's elimination and exercise needs. For play groups, the dogs go to a local dog park or contained area, and are able to run, bounce, play, and interact with other dogs. This has all the benefits of doggie daycare, without the steep impact to your wallet.

A group walk with one handler and up to two other dogs is a great way for less-exuberant dogs to get exercise, interact with other dogs, and enjoy the sunshine. Notice that I give the qualifier "up to two other dogs." If your dog-walker is walking 15 dogs, or really more than three at a time, you may wish to consider a different dog-walking service. I get concerned when a dog-walker has eight dogs on leash—I can vividly see a distraction causing all eight dogs to get tangled and pull the walker down on the pavement. Additionally, smaller dogs run the risk of getting trampled by larger dogs in the group, or there may be a slower dog that gets dragged along for his 20 minute break.

My rule of thumb is to consider what would happen in the event of an emergency? The more dogs that exist in a group means there is more opportunity for something to go awry, and if that happens, what happens to the other seven dogs when a single dog has to go to the veterinarian? Stick with services that promise attention to your dog, and only two additional buddies (maximum) for your dog to hang out with on group outings.

Solo Walks:

Dogs that need to get out but can't handle the proximity to other dogs, or who may be sick, recently had surgery, or are injured, slow down a group, or for whatever reason require one-on-one attention from a dog-walker, should investigate a solo-walk option. This is where your dog is the only dog being walked by a professional.

If your dog is reactive or aggressive to other dogs, a professional who is skilled at positive reinforcement techniques, Behavior Adjustment Training (BAT) certified, has a CPDT or other certification indicating they can handle reactive dogs is preferred. This way, your dog can get the training and space necessary to be successful on walks in the city, and you know your dog is being cared for appropriately. If you can't find a walker with these certifications for your stressed out dog, ask a local certified dog trainer whom they would recommend for reactive dogs. Make sure that this individual uses positive techniques instead of prongs and punishing techniques that can quickly elevate an overstimulated dog from mild reactivity to full out aggression, if not handled correctly.

This is the safest way to walk a group of dogs. There are almost as many people as dogs!
Photo submitted by Karen Harmin of Cambridge, MA.

What Do I Look For In A Playgroup or Dog-Walking Service?

Similar to a daycare, you want your provider to be fully insured, and bonded. They meet you and your dog prior to any walks and do a behavior assessment. You should show the service provider where the treats and poop bags are, a notepad for the provider to leave you any notes, and where the leash is located. They should provide you with a waiver and go over all of their expectations. Do you want to be called if Fluffy had an accident? At what point do you wish to be contacted for behavior, accidents, or incidents? Do you want a note every single day or just when something out of the ordinary happened on the outing? You should address any issues that need to be attended to, any special contingencies ("Rufus gets a peanut butter Kong after his walk"), and absolutely inquire about what you can expect from their services.

If the provider doesn't require a meeting first, or just takes your dog in a van with a dozen other dogs to a park, then I would strongly suggest another service provider. Most dog parks have a three-dog-to-person maximum, which makes sense. If your playgroup leader is taking more dogs than the park limits allow, then they are not paying as much attention to your dog, or respecting the rules of the city. Yes, it's a playgroup, so there should be some dogs around for your dog to play with, but if your provider has a dozen dogs, then the provider is only physically able to watch a couple at a time. Your dog might not be getting the attention you are paying for, or that provider might not be following the rules of the park (How can you pick up 12 dogs' poop if you can only watch a couple dogs at a time?).

Additionally, if one dog gets injured during play, how does that provider get the injured dog to the vet? The provider would have to take time to drop off 11 other dogs first. Take it one step further, and consider if that injured dog is yours—you don't want your dog waiting for medical attention. Make sure the provider is handling a safe number of dogs at a time, and that all city-wide regulations are being followed.

If a playgroup or dog-walking service determines that your dog isn't a good fit for their business model, or that your dog wouldn't be happy with the dogs in their care, it's ok. That provider is doing what they feel is in the best interest for the comfort level of your dog, as well as the other dogs in their group. If a dog doesn't fit well with the group energy, someone could get hurt. The provider should be able to make other recommendations for your dog, instead of leaving you high and dry. There is no one-size-fits-all business when it comes to dogs, and that's why there are so many options. Make sure you are finding the right professional and option for your budget and your dog's needs.

What If I Can't Take Fido With Me Overnight?

There are plenty of daycares and dog-walkers that will be able to take your dog if you have to go out of town for a night, or longer. Many of these businesses will only accept dogs that are current clients. The time to make arrangements for your dog for an overnight stay is not the day before you need to leave. Dogs have to be behaviorally tested to ensure that they are a good fit for the boarding facility or pet-sitter in advance.

My recommendation is to investigate overnight options relatively soon after the dog comes home. I get calls at least once a month from students asking if I take dogs overnight. Often, the conversation goes one of two ways:

Client: "Hi Melissa—We have to leave town. Do you take dogs overnight?"
Me: "No, sorry. I wish I could, but I can give you some people I trust!"
Client: "Great!"
Me: "Let me know when you're leaving, and how long you need your pet cared for?"
Client: "I'm leaving in a few days, and need care for the long holiday weekend."

Holiday weekends book up months in advance, so make sure you're one of the lucky ones to get coverage for your dog and call at least six weeks prior to your trip.

The second conversation tends to go like this:

Client: "Hi, Melissa. We've had a medical emergency in my family, and I have to get on a plane tonight. Can you take my dog?"
Me: "I'm so sorry—I can't take dogs, but I have a list of people I can recommend. Keep in mind they need to do a behavior evaluation first to make sure that your dog will be safe with their dogs, and they might be full. You might have to call someone to stay in your home. Do you have friends who can take your dog this time? If not, let me give you some names of people who can come into your home. Also, call your vets' office as they might have someone you already know who can come and stay, or take your pet this time."

In this case, which happens more often than anyone would like, the importance of being ready in the event of the unforeseen circumstance is illustrated. It's hard to find someone on a day's notice to come into your home, especially if you've never met this person before, assuming they are free to work that particular night. Additionally, it can be uncomfortable for you if you don't really know this person, and if your dog doesn't really know this person. It's a bit more risky. It's better to be safe than sorry, so start looking for overnight providers within a couple weeks of bringing a dog into the home.

What to Look For:
    For starters, know the basic laws. In many Massachusetts towns, a family can have up to three dogs without needing a kennel license. Pet sitters, because they tend to be people who love pets, often have one or two of their own dogs and as a result will be very selective of the dogs they take into their home. Some providers will have a kennel license and keep more than three dogs in their home, but they should have plenty of space, and the means of creating space for dogs that might be sensitive. In my home town in Maine, we had a dozen dogs and never needed a kenneling license for our pet dogs. Laws vary from state to state, and community to community. Regardless, a professional should never take on a dog that they feel upon evaluation cannot be managed, and comfortable, in their home.

"Oh, good. You brought room service!"
Violet is Kristin Barnes' muse and travel companion.

There are also dog hotels, with a variety of services (their own "room," a TV, and meals delivered to their door), boarding facilities (a line of cages where dogs have their own run, like a shelter), or daycares converted to overnight facilities (dogs play all day in the daycare, then someone stays overnight with the dogs that are kenneled in the evening). The possibilities are endless, and your dog's needs will be met, but it's just a matter of finding the right cost and environment for your dog. Make sure you have this provider lined up LONG before you need it, and book for busy weekends months in advance. My friend boards dogs in her home, and she has dogs over Thanksgiving break. She is often booked by September. Keep that in mind.

If My Dog Can't Be Around Other Dogs, What Do I Do?
This is a tricky circumstance. Most of the time we traveled to places where we could take our dogs with us. However, in a few cases (like our honeymoon, and later, the day we had our baby) we needed arranged care for the dogs. They each had different needs.

Our greyhound, Zeppelin, could hang out with any other dog, which made it much easier to find someone to take him. Our Border collie, Sadie, only enjoyed the company of our greyhound, which made things very difficult when arranging for her care. We had some friends stay in our home with Sadie, and sent our greyhound with his doggie friends, and that worked wonderfully. Everyone was fine and as an added bonus, our mail was brought in!

Some dog-walking services will have a staff member stay in a client's home. Others might have a staff member who can't own a dog, but is allowed a "visiting pet", where they can take a dog for a few nights. This would be a great option for people who can't put their dog in an environment with other dogs.

Call your veterinarians' office, the local pet boutique, or talk with your dog trainer. Many professionals in related industries board dogs in-home, or know people who can be recommended. The animal hospital I frequent has technicians who will travel to homes of clients for a little extra spending money, or as a side business. This is also a great option for dogs (and cats!) that need insulin, fluids, or other medical needs met while their owner is away. The added bonus is you can rest easy knowing that your pet is medically and emotionally cared for.

Final Thoughts:

It can be overwhelming to choose a provider for your dog. There are so many to select from when you live in the city. Talk to people who use these services, and do your homework. Make sure that the providers are smart, and that they take precautions to protect your dog and the other dogs in their care. If they ask you a lot of questions, give you an intake questionnaire, and conduct behavior evaluations, you can bet that they take their job seriously. These questions aren't to make your life more complicated, but to make sure that they are a good fit for you, and your dog will be a good fit for their existing clientele. It's up to you to make sure that these providers are insured, bonded, and trusted in your community. They should be as good with dogs as they are with people—bedside manner matters. As a last resort, trust your instincts. If you have a bad feeling about something, it's best to start over and find another provider who will suit you better.

*"Truman Coyote," afraid his dog-walker forgot him, decided to drive himself to the dog park.
He has a schedule that must be adhered to. There are butts to sniff, balls to chase, corners to
pee in…*
Karen Harmin used to live with this Border collie mix in California.

The Commandments of Working with a Service Provider:

- You need to share everything, *everything,* about your dogs with your provider, including that Sparky had French fries the night before, and that he once got away from you and disappeared for a week.
- You should have reasonable expectations of what a professional can accomplish in the limited time we spend with dogs. A trainer can only get so far, if you aren't putting in the time to work with your dog after a class. A dog-walker can give your dog a nice little outing, but your dog might still need to run with you when you get home. A groomer can only do a light trim if you are also brushing at home—otherwise, it's "Shave and a haircut-two bits!" A vet can only diagnose and give you a plan. It's up to you to follow the plan.
- If you are going to frequent dog parks and other dog recreation areas, you need to learn what constitutes healthy (and unhealthy) dog play. "Just let them work it out" works in some cases, but not all cases. If you want to study on your own, pick up Patricia McConnell's book on safe play[7] or look at Dr. Sophia Yin's website on safe dog park etiquette,[8] so you know when to intervene, when not to intervene, and how to diffuse a situation safely.
- You should be familiar with common illness that spread when dogs play in groups, like *giardia*, *coccidia*, papilloma and kennel cough. You should be aware of the symptoms of these common ailments, recognize them, know how to prevent them, and *report* them to your provider.
- Also, talk with a vet if your dog has diarrhea, signs of any skin infection, an ear infection, limping, and coughing. We are all service providers, but we aren't medical professionals, so please, please, please see your vet for any ailment. (I personally can't tell you how many times I've told students, "He's limping. I think it *might* be his knee, but you need to go to the vet," only to have it be the shoulder, the neck, a toe, and in one really bizarre case, an ear infection.) We can only tell you that something's wrong, but the vet can tell you what is wrong and how to fix it. We are all part of the same team. Put

---

[7] Patricia McConnell, *Off-Leash Dog Play: A Complete Guide to Safety and Fun!* (C&R Publishing, 2008).
[8] Sophia Yin, "Dog Park Etiquette: Rules to Help Dogs Get Along," August 23, 2012 (http://drsophiayin.com/blog/entry/dog-park-etiquette-rules).

another way—while Tom Brady is a great quarterback, he's not going to be an effective lineman. If you aren't sure if it's serious, call the animal hospital and talk with a technician prior to going in.

- If your dog has diarrhea, please don't bring it to the park, daycare, or participate in group activities.
- The same goes for pink-eye...
- ...and puppy warts.
- If you are calling a service provider into your home for help, please tell us in advance if the dog is going to jump on us, run away from us, bark at us, or try to eat us. It's just a nice thing to know walking in.
- You need to be willing to call Animal Control when a situation arises that poses a threat to other dogs or owners. Additionally, you need to know what information to get from another owner if your own dog gets attacked, or is the attacking dog. Being afraid of quarantine isn't a justifiable reason to NOT contact animal control. When in doubt, call.

Thanks to Pat Dains of On the Run, a dog playgroup service in Somerville, MA for helping me with this list!

Spay, Neuter, or Not?

In a sea of urban pet professionals, it's critical to talk with your vet about health

Once every class session, I'm asked by a student what my feelings are regarding spay or neuter. The short answer is quite simple: It's complicated.

For starters, there is a lot of information online. It can be daunting to go through, not all of it is correct, and some of it is incredibly outdated. It also depends on where the information is sourced. I focus on behavior and training, so most of my point of reference for suggesting surgical alteration comes from a training perspective. My vet friends advise on the latest information as it relates to health. Rescue and shelter groups don't want any more homeless pets overcrowding their shelters, so they would be inclined to spay as soon as possible. Breeders want your dog to look just the right way, breed for specific traits and possibly use a dog for showing or breeding; as a result, they might lean towards keeping the dogs intact much longer, or never altering the dog. Researchers want to discover important and interesting things, so they might have a different perspective entirely.

Information extracted from one expert might differ greatly from another expert. That being said, I've compiled a list that should help you make the best decision to spay or neuter, or not.

It's important to say that I am not a veterinarian and am not an expert in the medical field. I have consulted with several veterinarians in the last decade as a part of my work. As an extra precaution, I gave this chapter to two veterinarians for examination prior to putting this book in print. I feel capable of responsibly answering these specific questions as they relate to spay and neuter, but as always, when it comes to health, please seek the advice of your veterinarian.

Common Myths:
My dog will become fat and lazy if altered too early:

I hate to be the bearer of bad news, but your dog will be just as energetic post-op as he was pre-op. Case in point: my friend Matt and his neutered disc dog, One Eyed Jack, rocked the fields of the Northeast for several years. Jack beat out neutered and not-neutered dogs from all over the country. He was fast, skilled, neutered, and was also missing an eye. He competed in some of the highest levels of disc dog competition.

Jack didn't slow down for anyone, and he didn't have an ounce of fat on him.

If spaying or neutering calmed dogs down and made them lazy, I'd get a neutered Vizsla to fatten up, and hang out with on the sofa during football season, instead of the un-neutered Vizsla who requires 12 miles of aerobic activity every other day. In all seriousness, if you have an energetic dog, your dog will still be energetic after surgery.

"Cool, I'm ready for my date! Wait, we're going to the vet?
You're going to DO WHAT?!?"
Owned by Maureen O'Connor; photo by Melissa Mullen Photography

This myth stems from the timing of the surgery. Spay and neuter procedures traditionally occur around six months of age, though these recommendations are changing. At around six months of age, your puppy is also starting to mature a little bit more, and has different needs than he did as a rambunctious three-month old. He will still have boundless energy, though it's teenager energy instead of baby energy.

When dogs become fat, it's usually because they are overfed, or maybe have other medical issues that need to be addressed, so talk with your vet. Also consider that their energy needs change over time, just like ours. If a dog is less active, then it requires less food, end of story. If the dietary changes aren't made, or exercise needs change for a particular pet due to injury, age, health, or work schedules, then the dog becomes overweight.

My female dog HAS to have a litter or heat cycle before she's spayed:
This used to be more a common rationale to delay spaying pets, though it still comes up from time to time. I heard one of my favorite podcasters talking about how this was recommended to him in the Pacific Northwest, which was incredibly frustrating to hear. The theory is that having a litter of puppies calms the dog down and matures her. This

is especially frustrating when medical professionals and behavior theorists have been working hard on debunking this myth. On average, a female dog will have her first cycle between six and fifteen months of age. By the time the dog has her first litter, she is more mature, regardless of whether she had a litter or not.

Many veterinarians also suggest that the spay occur before the first heat cycle, because each cycle they have increases the likelihood of mammary cancer, as well as a higher risk of pregnancy. The risk of pyometra (a nasty, sudden infection of the uterus that can be fatal) increases the longer a female remains intact.

Lastly, as much as you think your dog would be a "great mom," "a wonderful stud," or the puppies would be so very cute, this single statistic should bring you back to reality: 4-6 million pets are euthanized each year, because they are homeless and our shelters are overcrowded.

Let's repeat that. 4-6 million pets are euthanized every single year.

According to The Humane Society of the United States, street dogs aren't the only dogs that are reproducing. These statistics also factor in the loved pets, including purebred dogs, who find themselves in shelters all across the America. In the United States, one cat or dog is killed in a shelter every single second.

For all the people who love the animals that are in your home, let me applaud you, because only one pet in ten finds a permanent, lifetime home. Don't add to the population problem, no matter how cute the puppies would be. As you can see from the stats, people breed dogs because they love the breed and do so responsibly, but there are others who breed dogs because they'd be cute, they try to make a quick buck, or there was a "whoops" with the Labrador next door. Not all dogs go to good homes. If they did, shelters wouldn't be overcrowded across the country. There are far too many cute puppies that need help immediately.

Now, go give your dog (or cat) a big hug. I just did.

Our kids should witness the miracle of birth:
I had a student tell me this once. They wanted to breed their dog so their children could witness the miracle of birth. I'm a huge advocate of hands-on education, but that's no reason to have your dog go through the stress of pregnancy. I personally had a baby because I wanted to be

a mom, not so my husband could "witness the miracle of birth." There are YouTube videos for that type of self-education.

What most people don't realize is that stress starts at mating. The male and female get "stuck" together during sex to allow the semen ample opportunity to do what it needs to do. This is really difficult to explain to young children—trust me, I was once that kid who walked in on our huskies "stuck" together, and my poor dad had never been so tongue-tied.

Some females will kill and eat the young that are sick and unhealthy; some pups are stillborn, and others die shortly after birth. That's not exactly *witnessing the miracle of life*. It's nature at its rawest, and it's really hard to explain to a kid why there were five puppies, and now only four.

Many people think that breeders make a ton of money on a litter, considering the cost of a purebred puppy. LearnToBreed.com has a fantastic breakdown of what goes into producing a healthy litter, and how to do so ethically. It's staggeringly expensive, and you're lucky if you break even because of the vaccines, deworming, costs of a whelping box, special lights, costs to ensure that the breeding dogs are healthy, stud fees, and other considerations that really pile up. You have to do it out of love, not for any dues you owe your dog, or your kids.

You'd be better off renting *Porky's* and explaining the birds and the bees that way, or watching YouTube videos of birth. If it's not fun for you to watch *The Miracle of Life*, it's not going to be fun for your kid watching it with you, and it's not fair to have your dog be their teacher.

Other Reasons To Consider Spay/Neuter:

According to Dr. Nicholas Dodman of Tufts University, neutering a dog can reduce his tendency to roam by 90%[9]. Translation: If he has no junk, he has no reason to look for hotties, and therefore he won't be as likely to be hit by a car in search of a nice piece of tail. Ask your veterinarian friends how many dogs are brought in as HBC's (hit-by-car) per year. The numbers are really gut-wrenching, and they will tell you that these dogs tend to have church-bells for testicles. They needed to roam and suffered, often fatally, for it.

- Neutering a dog significantly reduces awkward leg-humping of

[9] Dodman, Nicholas, *Sexual Behavior in Dogs*, PetPlace http://www.petplace.com/article/dogs/behavior-training/normal-behavior/sexual-behavior-in-dogs / (April 8, 2015).

guests, especially if the dog is neutered before he reaches sexual maturity.

- The procedure reduces fixation in dog-to-dog interactions, where a dog gets fixated on one dog to the point of compulsion. This is frequently observed at dog parks and in larger groups of dogs.
- Inappropriate marking is less likely when the dog is neutered before puberty, and proper house-training techniques are applied.
- Cryptorchid dogs, dogs whose testicles haven't descended, tend to have a higher rate of tumor growth in the undescended testicles. It's recommended that these dogs get neutered.
- Spaying a female *eliminates* the possibility of uterine cancer, ovarian cancer, and cervical cancer.
- Spayed females have a drastically reduced chance of developing mammary (breast) cancer.
- Spayed females won't bleed all over your house for 10 days straight twice a year.
- Spayed and neutered animals have cheaper pet licensing fees in most communities.
- Spaying *eliminates* the risk of pyometra, an infection of the uterus which is similar to appendicitis in that the infection is sudden, it's expensive to treat, and if left untreated, is fatal. According to the ASPCA, the risk is upwards of 25% in female dogs[10] that are not spayed.
- If your dog is an unaltered male, he won't be allowed in daycares, playgroups or public dog parks after six months of age, on average. If your female is unaltered, she won't be allowed in these facilities while she's in heat.

Keep in mind that not all of our canine problems are solved easily with a snip. If your dog has a tendency to mark in the house, getting him neutered might not solve the problem, but it may help you get the behavior under control in combination with training. I know many male dogs that were neutered before sexual maturity that still hump and mount dogs at the park, but many of them have figured out that it's a quick way to get another dog to play chase. "I mount them and they chase me—yay playtime!"

You will still have to train your dog to get the behaviors you dislike

---

[10] ASPCA, *Unspayed Pets Susceptible to Potentially Fatal Infections, Massive Swelling,* https://www.aspca.org/blog/unspayed-pets-susceptible-potentially-fatal-infections-massive-swelling (January 14, 2015).

under control in tandem with the neuter. The longer a dog remains intact, the harder it is for sexually related behaviors to cease, especially if those sexually related behaviors have become behavioral patterns. Some classic examples of these more challenging behaviors include humping (people and dogs), and territorial marking, which will take some time to get under control.

Aggression in males tends not to be cured with a neuter, but aggression can certainly be fueled by hormones as a dog ages, so it's best to alter your dog before puberty for the best chance to reduce aggressive tendencies.

Risks of Spaying/Neutering:

As with any surgical procedure, there are risks related to adverse reactions to anesthesia, infection, and other complications; however, for spays and neuters, the instances of serious complications are *extremely* low.

The biggest difference in neutered and unneutered dogs (aside from the obvious missing testicles) is that the growth plates close sooner in unneutered dogs. As a result, unneutered dogs tend to have bigger muscles and more angled heads, thanks to extra testosterone closing those growth plates and adding extra "oomph" to the rest of the animal. Dogs neutered before adolescence tend to have longer legs, flatter chests, and rounder faces. These are mostly aesthetic issues, though there are some scientific studies in the works that are addressing whether or not there is any concern other than aesthetic value.

There are higher instances of bladder incontinence in spayed females. However, the occurrences of mild incontinence is highest in really early spay procedures (prior to three months of age). Incontinence, while inconvenient, can be treated in many cases and is not a life threatening condition, unlike cancer.

There have been reported joint problems due to the hormones responsible for closing growth plates being absent or minimized. This is more of a concern for dogs actively competing in sports, and giant breed dogs. Discuss with your veterinarian if you plan to be competitive with your dog, or if you have a large breed dog. Regardless of the spay/neuter question as it relates to joint issues, make sure that your large-breed puppy is on an appropriate diet for large-breed puppies. This will help with the joint issues cited in some studies.

Bone Cancer and Hypothyroidism

When I'm asked by my students about spay and neuter, I speak as a trainer and a behavior evaluator. My goal is to make sure I am doing right by my profession, the dogs I work with, and their families. When I'm asked my opinion if a family should have their dog fixed, my standard response is "ask your vet what they suggest, as this is a medical issue. However, my recommendation lines up with most of the vets I've ever visited or consulted with. In order to head off certain behavior and health problems, have your pet spayed or neutered prior to six months of age." I also add that there are vets who recommend surgery at four months of age for faster recovery rates (they wake up, roll over, and eat!), but that conversation needs to happen with the veterinarian.

Occasionally, I'm presented with, "But my breeder said...", or "I read online that..." Without fail, I am handed a study that proves that cancer, or hypothyroidism, or some other horrible, terrible disease is killing dogs, and it's because they were sexually altered.

There is one study that has been handed to me, linked in an email, or cited by students more frequently than any other. It states, definitively, that dogs that are neutered or spayed have higher rates of bone cancer. This is true, if you only read a part of the study, but there is a bit more to it than "sexual alteration will give my dog bone cancer." What the study states is this:

"...the risk of osteosarcoma rose with increasing age, increasing body weight, increasing standard weight and increasing standard height...the highest risk of osteosarcomas was found for large and giant breeds, while small breeds had reduced risks. A twofold excess risk was observed among neutered dogs. [The study] showed a stronger and more consistent association of osteosarcoma with increasing height than increasing weight."[11]

There is an increase in bone cancers in dogs that are neutered, but taking the whole picture into account, there is a greater likelihood of osteosarcoma in taller, bigger dogs—which, we've known for years are the dogs that are prone to this type of cancer; being neutered increases this already higher risk in larger dogs specifically. These dogs include Rottweilers, Great Danes, greyhounds, and dogs with larger body types

---

[11] Ru, Terracinni and Glickman (1998). Host related risk factors for canine osteosarcoma. *Veterinary Journal.* Jul;156(1):31-9

and longer leg bones. I would like to interject that while the risk of osteosarcoma is higher for these dogs, the overall risk factors for an early demise including hit by car, pyometra, mammary cancer, and other risks for not having the spay or neuter done is much, much, much greater.

The other condition that has been cited by students as a reason to avoid sexually altering pets is hypothyroidism. In short, hypothyroidism is when the thyroid isn't producing enough hormone. There are many symptoms linked to this hormone imbalance, including skin issues, weight issues, and hair loss. Hypothyroidism has been documented in *one* study as being higher in cases where the animal was sexually altered.

"Neutered male and spayed female dogs had a higher relative risk of developing hypothyroidism than did sexually intact females. Sexually intact females had a lower relative risk. Breeds with a significantly increased risk, compared with other breeds, were the Doberman Pinscher and Golden Retriever."[12]

The above quote is from a study that is still occasionally sent to me in support of not spaying or neutering dogs. It's important to note that this study was conducted from 1987-1992. That's 23 years ago—that study is old enough for a pub crawl. There have been few studies since that I could easily find that even bring up thyroid, and it turns out that the reason I couldn't find any more supporting data is that there is none. I emailed Dr. Laurie Siperstein-Cook of the SPCA at Sacramento, and she explained that, "More recent and larger studies have *not* found a relationship between spay/neuter and hypothyroidism...recent review papers on risks and benefits of spay/neuter in vet journals hardly ever mention hypothyroidism."

The dogs that had the highest risk of hypothyroidism post-neuter in this study were golden retrievers and Doberman pinschers, which are consistently among the top dog breeds to be affected by hypothyroidism anyway. In short, regardless of whether you alter your retriever or not, you will have an increased risk of hypothyroidism, not because you altered your dog, but because you have a golden retriever.

---

12 Panciera DL. (1994). Hypothyroidism in dogs: 66 cases (1987-1992). *Journal of the American Veterinary Association.* Mar 1;204(5):761-7

Science!

I mention the above two examples to highlight a bigger point, not to upset veterinarians who are reading this and might wonder why I'm bringing up these particular studies. If your breeder gave you literature on why you shouldn't have your pet fixed, feel free to read it critically, but also have a discussion with the medical professional who is caring for you and your dog. It's also best to have this discussion with your vet instead of asking your dog trainer who, as I state again (even after diving down some very interesting rabbit holes to write this chapter) is not a vet, nor qualified to give medical advice. If I'm not in a position to give advice ethically without checking my sources and vetting my writing with veterinarians, and I work with animals every single day of my life, then please don't accept everything you read on the internet, advice from "that guy at the dog park", a breeder who is not a vet, a person who transports dogs for rescue, a dog groomer, daycare provider, or anyone other than a trusted professional who has a medical degree. I have worked with dozens of veterinarians at various animal hospitals all over the Metro-Boston region. The overwhelming majority of these professionals are looking at the science and really do have your pet's best interest at heart.

If you are going to look at data online and find sources to back up your position, make sure you are looking at reliable resources. Are the stories anecdotal or are they backed in scientific journals? Have the studies been replicated, or not, like the hypothyroid study I still get after 23 years? What does your vet think? Personally, I find it's much better, and easier, to just go talk to the professional who earned a degree in the field relating to the health of your dog. As demonstrated above, you can find a blurb or a study to back up almost any position, but can you find other scientific studies that replicate the data?

Lastly, think about what the article or study is stating. If I know I can prevent pyometra in my dog, and prevent mammary cancer, ovarian cancer, uterine cancer and cervical cancer, but she might have a slightly increased risk of hypothyroidism, I'm going to roll the dice on her needing thyroid meds later in life, and stop cancer in its track. Additionally, if a cancer risk is "doubled" from 1% to 2% with spay and neuter, or even 4%-8%, that's still a *92% chance she's not going to get that cancer*. I'll roll those dice any day of the week. That's still a very small chance that she'll get a cancer that is correlated with spay and neuter, (though no cancers are proven to be caused by it), and a 100% chance she won't get the other cancers I know are prevented. I feel pretty good about those numbers.

Look at all the facts as they are presented, look at the numbers as they are presented, don't be scared by sensational terms like "double-risk" without knowing what specific number is doubled, and you guessed it—talk with your vet.

Pediatric Spay and Neuter: Is it Safe?

Whatever the feeling on sexual alterations of pet dogs, pediatric spay and neuter (surgical sterilization prior to six months of age as defined by the ASPCA) seems to have the biggest push back, though in shelters, it's a necessary procedure. As a means of keeping the population down, these dogs are altered as soon as possible, in some cited cases as early as six-eight weeks of age.

If you already have a dog and elect to have early spay/neuter performed, it's advised to talk with your veterinarian. Many veterinarians support early spay and neuter, as early as four months of age. The dogs that have the procedure done at that age literally wake up, start eating and playing after the surgery. The recovery time is remarkably fast. Others prefer the more traditional age of six months. Either way, every veterinarian I talked with recommends that pet dogs are spayed and neutered *prior* to puberty, and the earlier the procedure is done, the better chance of heading off several of the behaviors and medical issues listed at the beginning of this chapter.

Groups such as the Humane Society of the United States, the ASPCA, American Animal Hospital Association, American Kennel Club, and the California Veterinary Medical Association all have endorsed pediatric spay and neuter. There has been a growing body of evidence to support pediatric spay and neuter over the last two decades. However, the debate still goes on in part because there are behavior specialists who are chiming in with behavior issues that still need to be studied, and there are still breeders out there who contractually do not allow spay and neuter of the dogs that are placed with families (and a rare few using 23-year-old studies to support their position). And then, there is the internet debate on everything, including if the earth is round.

That said, if you still have reservations about pediatric spay and neuter, or reservations regarding a shelter performing this procedure, know this: Most communities and states have mandatory spay/neuter prior to adoption and for good reason. For them, the pros of alteration far outweigh the chance that one of their dogs will have six more that will end up in a shelter that is already over capacity. The dogs that are spayed and neutered have a much longer life expectancy overall, compared to dogs that have not had the procedure done. Period.

In Conclusion: To Alter, or Not?

Our 80-pound greyhound that was neutered at three years old was always at a higher risk of developing bone cancer than our 40-pound Border collie, who was spayed at four months old in a shelter. Even though he was neutered really late, he wasn't safe from a cancer that has killed at least six greyhounds that I knew personally in the last decade, including him. Regardless of whether or not Zeppelin was neutered, the chances he would succumb to osteosarcoma were so high, that I had a talk with my husband about it prior to adopting the dog. I can say with relative confidence that his testicles, whether present or absent, would likely not have changed the outcome. He still statistically would have had cancer and died as a result of it, not because he was neutered, but because he was a greyhound.

The rescue group had Zeppelin neutered before he came to us. If it were up to me, I'd still go ahead and have the surgery performed. Behavior is worth it to me, and I feel that he lived a happier life not dealing with behavioral issues that were curbed with a routine procedure. I was happier knowing my boy wasn't planning his escape to knock up the intact pit bull down the street twice a year. Besides, I've actually met a pit-greyhound mix and it was one of the strangest things that I've ever seen. She was like a wiggly muscular sausage with a narrow head and very skinny legs.

You might make a different decision entirely, but make sure that the decision you make is an informed one and that you are asking the right reputable professionals. Make sure you aren't making a decision based on something that you saw on the internet that can't be substantiated. There are veterinarians who support spay and neuter, and others who do not support spay and neuter. Find out why they feel the way they do, have them give you literature on the subject from medical journals, and make an informed decision.

Think critically about any study you read. Just like with human studies, one day coffee is bad for you, the next day it will add 75 years to your life. You have to ask yourself what is the study trying to prove? How old is the study? What does your vet say, who is hopefully up to date on the latest scientific data? What issues are you having with your dog? What breed is your dog, and what health issues are related to that particular breed? Are you in an area where your dog can knock up the poodle next door, creating the ill-advised "shar-poodle"? Is the obsessive leg humping worth not neutering your mastiff so he can have a big blocky head? Can you deal with a 200-pound dog with an embarrassing leg-humping problem?

Make a list of pros and cons. Look at the big picture instead of focusing on one statistic. Figure out what will be best for your family, and ultimately for your dog. And, for Dog's sake, talk with your veterinarian.

Ditch the Dish!

Mental stimulation, what it is, and why it's critical for urban dogs

Cities are wonderful if you love the hustle and bustle of it all. There is a lot to do for a person in the city, but while you're out on Newbury Street with friends, your dog is home and likely bored out of his mind. As a result, many city-dwellers have to work much harder to find outlets for urban hounds, lest they come home to a torn up sofa, or worse.

According to the ASPCA, feral and wild dogs spend 80% of their waking time scavenging, hunting, and looking for food[13]. Look around and see what your dog is doing at this moment. My wager is that your dog is lying around, jumping up on someone for attention, or chewing on something. If you are lucky, it's an item appropriate for dog use. Dogs are naturally active, social and cerebral creatures, and we are doing them no service by leaving them in an apartment building by themselves all day long. Unless he's eating, playing with you, or sleeping, he's very likely bored which can lead to a slew of problems that are many times totally preventable or manageable with the right balance of exercise, mental stimulation and quiet time.

To make things more challenging in an urban environment, many of us live in apartments with thin walls, neighbors that are six feet away, or have landlords who live downstairs. Brakes squeal, garbage cans fall over, and kids play in the street. All of these things grab at the attention of a dog that is looking for something to do. A barking dog, no matter the reason, is hard on everyone who can hear the dog, especially in urban centers.

Many boredom issues can be helped significantly with a job to do. Purebred dog owners should understand that their dog was bred for a specific task. Typically, these tasks involve complex thought processes and decision making skills, as well as a certain degree of aerobic activity. Today's Labrador retrievers and Jack Russell terriers have deep historical roots where their ancestors had to do a job to survive.

Even the greyhound is still used for hunting in some parts of the country. Pet dogs still need to experience similar exercise and mental stimulation as their ancestors did, or at least we need to trick the system into thinking that it's doing similar work. The greyhound does this by

---

[13] ASPCA *Enriching Your Dog's Life* https://www.aspca.org/pet-care/virtual-pet-behaviorist/dog-behavior/enriching-your-dogs-life

chasing a mechanical bunny on a track for sport. Ethics aside, the greyhounds on the track really think they are going to get the bunny and centuries of breeding for a heightened prey drive kicks in as soon as the race-gates open. They tricked the system in these dogs, for sport.

Take my dog, Sadie, for example. She was a Border collie that, for better or worse, lived in a congested city. If she didn't have a job to do, then she likely would have destroyed my living space, or barked excessively, leading to our eviction. It was up to me to make sure that she had her high-energy needs met. Most dog owners at least know they should do this. Owners take high-energy dogs for runs, engage in playtime, and take them on hikes—but they are often missing a very critical piece of the puzzle.

Like most urban dogs, Karl Barx prefers to be with his owner, Polina Stolyar, even if that means he has to hang up his rat catching tendencies for a paddle down the Charles River. Don't let his small size fool you – he's an energetic guy!

In addition to exercise, dogs have to be mentally engaged in some meaningful way. While Sadie was home during the day, she needed to have *something to do*. We didn't have sheep, cows, or goats, and I really didn't want her herding the cats or the baby. We had to come up with a few outlets that satisfied her need for mental engagement as well as physical activity. Some of these activities are more creative than others, but they were mandatory and were part of her routine. When you live in the city, dog responsibility goes beyond feeding, walking, and picking up dog poop. When you live in the city, exercise might be harder to get. You can't just let your dog run freely through the streets of Boston! Aerobic activity might be more expensive if daycare is the only option for your dog. Even with aerobic activity, mental stimulation is an absolute must. You might need to be creative, especially if your dog needs physical space, or is still in training.

Dogs Need To Work Their Brains, Too!

I used to stand in a field and throw a flying disc or a ball to Sadie for three hours, which was three hours that I had my active dog outside and working, in addition to her morning and afternoon walks; but it was also three hours out in the frigid New England weather in December. I hate the cold, she loved the cold, so Houston, we had a problem.

The better alternative was to make her *work* for her toy. I'd have her leap over my legs, sit, stay, and spin before getting the disc. I'd put together little routines to make her work for that prized flying plastic. In addition, I was playing with my dog, building a complex communication model with my dog, and we were a team. Before this, I was just a means of her getting a toy. I stood in a field and tossed a toy, toss and stand, toss and stand. I was so bored and was not really a part of the game. As we built our ability to play together, her exercise needs actually *decreased*. Instead of needing a three hour chunk of time every day to burn her energy, she would go for a couple of 20 minute walks through the day and work for an hour aerobically with mental stimulation. Overall, she was happier, and so was I. This was much better, not only for her, but for my social life!

Another tip that made Sadie a better roommate was eliminating her food dish. This is something I recommend to almost all of my students when I go into their homes. Think of it like this: Your dog can eat in 30 seconds, and then come begging you for entertainment, which is a relatively common scenario. Alternatively, your dog can work for his breakfast over the course of 20 minutes by using a food dispensing toy after you leave for work. This technique staves off boredom, while keeping your dog mentally engaged on something other than you, or your absence.

There are hundreds of toys out there designed to keep dogs mentally engaged while working for their food, and thousands of ways to use things around the house to keep your dog occupied mentally.

Kongs® and Other Mentally Stimulating Toys:

Everyone has heard of the Kong® toy, but to make this toy even more challenging for your high-energy dog, fill the Kong® with cream cheese, yogurt or peanut butter. Then, take a dog biscuit and shove it into the soft substance in the Kong®. Freeze the toy, and when you need a distraction, you have one ready to go.

After I had our baby, I purchased ten of these beautiful, magic toys. I put them in an egg carton in the freezer (see below, and don't judge me for the pre-made sweet potato casserole—it's delicious). Once a week, I mixed kibble with cream cheese, peanut butter or soft dog food, stuffed the toys, and stored them in the freezer. I could nurse my baby in peace, while the dogs worked contentedly on their frozen breakfast. Everyone was happy and working on an activity.

I continued this practice with Sadie, who was 12 years old. Exercise became tough on her after developing arthritis and vision problems. These food toys gave her such great joy, and kept her entertained a couple of times daily.

Pro Tip: Use an egg carton in the freezer to store stuffed toys and freeze them upright. This is a cheap storage option and much less mess!

Additional toys include the Kong Genius™ series, the Busy Buddy Linkables™ series and the Omega Paw Tricky Treat Ball™. All of these toys are great for dogs that enjoy tossing toys around the home to get their food. All of the toys listed above are hard rubber toys that bounce unpredictably, while protecting hardwood floors. The Genius™ and Linkable™ toys are designed to fit together with other pieces from the series to vary the difficulty of the toy, so things stay interesting for the dog and human spectators. The Treat Ball™ doesn't have that functionality, but it's a great starter purchase for dogs just learning to work for their food.

The Bob-A-Lot™ and the Kong Wobbler™ are two toys that are hard plastic and great for beginners. Kibble is poured into the toy through a screw top lid. These toys are weighted at the bottom, and narrow on the top. Screw the toy back together, and watch the dog get the pieces of kibble out of the toy by punching it with his nose or paw. Because these toys are weighted at the bottom and narrow at the top, every time the toy is pushed, it springs back upright, like a punch-me-clown! To make these toys harder, you can eventually add a small ball to block the hole where kibble comes out so the dog has to hit the toy at certain angles to be successful.

Ken and Andy Mallon of Medford, Massachusetts, feed Callie every meal out of puzzle toys. These toys keep her entertained, and slow down her eating.

Nina Ottosson is famous for creating toys that engage a dogs' brain with puzzles. Some of these puzzle toys are easy, some are really challenging, and others have multiple functionalities to keep your dog guessing for long periods of time. Her series of toys are great for dogs that like to dig and constantly use their brain to get into trouble. Sadie liked to toss toys instead of poke them, so these weren't the best options for her, but your dog might love to use his paw or nose to move puzzle pieces for hidden food.

You don't have to spend a lot of money on toys. If you have a fenced-in back yard, or a long line and a little time to kill, you can scatter the breakfast portion of your dog's food in the grass, and have him "hunt" for kibble or cheese bits. While your dog isn't running around and aerobically burning off energy, he is sniffing and using his brain to find food. Many dogs will settle down nicely after searching for breakfast!

Other ideas:
- Fill a hard plastic kiddie pool with water. Dice up a hot dog, and let your pup "bob for hot dogs." This is a great game in the summer when it might be too hot for aerobic activity, but you need to do something with your dog before you both go crazy.
- Get a hard plastic kiddie pool, and fill it with sand. Hide a few toys, milk bones, or a frozen stuffed toy for your pup to find. This is a great outlet for dogs that like to dig (I'm looking at you, dachshund owners).
- Put your dog's kibble in a metal bowl. Pour water or chicken broth over it, and freeze. When you're ready, give the dog his food dish and let him work for his kibble. You can also hide toys, frozen stuffed Kongs®, carrot pieces, and other goodies in the ice! This is an activity best suited for outdoor recreation, or in an area you don't mind cleaning up later. This is a trick shelters do to mentally enrich dogs in the kennels without spending a lot of money.
- You can also put kibble in a small box. If your dog is ambitious, you can close the box and let Fido try to open his "present". If your dog prefers to throw things around, you can cut small holes in the box to allow random pieces of food to fall out during play. In the event your dog just likes to dig, you can put the box over a pile of food and let the dog knock the box over. You can really cater this idea to the type of dog you have and the kind of play they enjoy!
- When you leave for work, hide a few treats around the apartment and hide a puzzle toy for your pup to find during your absence.

Malcolm keeping cool and staying busy in a hard plastic kiddie pool!
Owned by Jackie Johnson, Washington D.C.

If you are active on social media, you might have seen a horrible story suggesting that ice can "cause stomach spasms that might kill your dog." This circulates every year on social media. This myth has been debunked by several top veterinarians all over the country[14]. If you see something on the internet, make sure you check for sources. Remember that anecdotal evidence, or sample sizes of one, does not make an epidemic. It doesn't matter how sad the story happens to be or how many times the story is re-tweeted. It's on you to do your research and investigate if a story is truthful, or in the case of ice cubes killing a dog, a bit suspect. If it sounds sensational, it very likely is.

You can look up "shelter enrichment" for more ideas that are economical, fun, and mentally engaging for your particular dog, or find activities that are linked to her genetic background. If you have a scenting dog, have her search for puzzle toys or kibble. If you have a dog that likes to run, have her chase each piece of food. If you have a brainiac, have her work for dinner by learning new tricks. There are so many ways to build the relationship with your dog without breaking the bank.

---

[14] Joanna Prisco, *Will Ice Cubes and Ice Water Kill Your Dog This Summer?*, ABC News, http://abcnews.go.com/Lifestyle/truth-ice-water-dogs/story?id=24231633 (June 20, 2014).

Keep in mind:

Anything you do for your dog to stay mentally engaged is going to help with many common problem behaviors. Boredom, intensity, exercise, and anxiety are all helped by adding puzzle toys and mental stimulation as part of a daily routine. These toys and games don't fix everything, but they help reduce enough stress that shelters are now using them with great effect, to help homeless dogs cope in a stressful environment. Trainers, behavior consultants and vet behaviorists are using these methods to help create structure and engage dogs in a new way. Besides, these games and toys are so much fun for your dog, why wouldn't you use them?

Sports!

Come for the exercise; stay for the impulse control

Why Aerobic Activity is Important for Urban Dogs:

Exhibit A: This is why aerobic activity is important for urban dogs.
Thanks for the demo, Archie! Photo taken by David Harmin

We've all heard that dogs will find a job if they aren't given one. What does that mean exactly? On the surface, dogs are animals that need to have exercise, social experiences, and mental stimulation. Think for one minute about what might happen to dogs that are taken from the environments they were bred for. Consider their genetic predisposition to work, run, play, engage, hunt, and roam. Now put that same dog in a city with leash laws, concrete, limited time outdoors, way more stimulation, and fewer coping mechanisms. I saw the *Beverly Hillbillies* and am a fan of the "fish out of water" genre, but when it comes to our dogs, there is a lot more at stake. The further we take dogs out of their environment, the harder we have to work to supplement their nature as dogs. We owe them that much.

At best, the "work" these dogs will take on frustrates their owners. At worst, it can be downright dangerous. For example, without appropriate outlets for their herding instinct, cattle dogs might be inclined to collect children by nipping at their heels. This behavior might be funny on the surface. I've seen dozens of these dogs on YouTube, so people do think it's amusing. I was even asked by a television producer if I would be interested in teaching a Border collie to "collect" kids to help a mom babysit her children. What could *possibly* go wrong? Dogs need outlets, but when we play these scenarios out, it's really only a matter of time before a kid gets bitten because the dog thought it was doing its job. Terriers tend to dig and bark. Retrieving dogs put things in their mouths, and will chew, digest and shred everything—dog toys and expensive shoes alike (did you say Jimmy Chews? Don't mind if I do!) Guarding dogs will often stare out of windows and bark at every passer-by, rustling leaf, or poor unsuspecting mail-delivery professional.

Like humans, dogs need an appropriate outlet for their stress and pent-up energy. Without one, they will deal with those feelings the only way they know how, based on the characteristics of their breed, and they aren't wrong to do so. They're simply responding to what comes naturally to them. If denied an appropriate outlet for too long, one bad behavior might lead to several. This compounding effect is one reason many dogs end up in shelters: They act in ways compatible with being a dog, but if left unchecked, these same behaviors become incompatible with human social constructs. No one wants a barking dog. Or a digging dog. Or a growling dog. No one wants personal belongings chewed. When dogs are bored or dissatisfied, they tend to bark, dig, jump, growl or chew. The result is a communication breakdown between the species.

When puppies display bad manners we tend to give them a pass, because they're just puppies. However, as they mature into adult dogs, our ability to forgive that same behavior wanes. When I go into a home, it's not uncommon for me to hear, "He knows he shouldn't jump", or, "She keeps peeing in the corner, and she knows better." I don't know about you, but I was no picnic as a teenager. I made some awful decisions, even though I "knew better". As dogs navigate adolescence on their way to adulthood, they need our help, even more so than when they are puppies.

Like their human counterparts, adolescent dogs (aged six to twenty-four months) make a LOT of mistakes. They test boundaries, forget basic commands, and often behave in surprisingly frustrating ways. Where did my adorable puppy go and who is this dog standing in front of me?

Based on what we know from studying humans, making mistakes is a critical part of the learning experience during adolescence, and that same concept is true for all mammals. As any parent of a teenager can attest, this can be the most frustrating time, and the same goes for our pups. In the United States alone, the shelter system is overrun with dogs in this age group; many surrendered because the owner believes the dog has behavior problems, but upon further evaluation, we find that a large population of these dogs suffer from a lack of training or access to suitable outlets for their natural drives. Maybe they weren't matched with the right family to begin with, or perhaps their puppy training wasn't enough to help them cope during the difficult period of adolescence.

When dogs start engaging in unwanted behaviors, they are begging for something to do with their instinctive programming. You can't necessarily train a beagle to stop scenting, a Nova Scotia duck toller to stop jumping, or a dachshund to stop barking; however, you can learn to manage behaviors by controlling them within certain parameters, and use those behaviors to help your dog cope in a structured way.

"Alo" taking his owner, Daniel Lampke for a run over the River Charles

Many behavior problems are easily addressed by taking a positive reinforcement class or giving the dog a job to do. But what if you don't have access to sheep in the city? What if it's not kosher for your terrier to actually get the city rats? If you live in our city, the rats are bigger than most of the dogs designed for vermin-work! Are you the owner of a truffle hunter, but not a truffle in sight? (Hello to all the Lagotto Romagnolo owners).

There is good news. If you have a legitimate behavior problem, there are resources for you (IAABC.org, among others included in a later chapter). If your dog is just simply acting out or engaging in behaviors typical of most adolescent dogs, there is very likely help in your city. Many urban environments have training centers that incorporate dog sports into their curriculum. This can significantly reduce boredom in dogs, and give owners an activity to do with their best friend. These classes help owners learn how to handle a dog off-leash, tire the dog physically, and provide critical mental stimulation. Everyone benefits! You benefit by strengthening the bond with your dog. The community benefits by having fewer barking and unsatisfied dogs.

In our area, there are canine disc, agility, Earthdog™ and Nose Work™ classes, as well as clubs for Flyball, tracking, dock diving, competition obedience, rally, and freestyle/dog dance. Other cities have similar outfits, and other activities. You just have to know where to look, and what you're looking for.

Shale likes to take her owner, Karen Bernstein, out for long walks on the beach – If by "long walks on the beach" you mean "throw the #*$^ disc."

Disc Dog

This is my baby. I love the sport of disc dog. If you call it Frisbee™ we'll forgive you, but for trademark reasons, the F-word is banned.

If you have an energetic, highly motivated, dog that loves to chase or fetch, you can't get much more fun for your buck than this. It's relatively inexpensive, and you can do it in a small space if you work lots of flips, impulse control, and short throws. If you're fortunate enough to have access to a big field in the city, you can let your dog run after long throws. Either way, it's great exercise and fantastic mental stimulation for the dog.

The impulse control your dog gets out of disc and other sports is an added bonus. If your dog is a jumper, providing an outlet for jumping (jumping for a disc) while disallowing jumping in every other context (on grandma) is an excellent way to curb unwanted behaviors.

You can play in your backyard after work with dog-specific discs (never human discs—they can shatter and cause injury), or you can join a club where you can hang out with other disc dog enthusiasts. Some communities have disc dog classes and clubs. If you prefer a crowd, you can show off freestyle routines (choreographed maneuvers with the dog and discs, with leg-weaves, and body vaults all set to music) or participate in dozens of other games. Distance/Accuracy is a timed event where a dog and handler get points based on how far down a field a dog can make a catch. Frizzgility is a Frisbee™ and agility combo sport which is as much fun to play as it is to watch. Extreme Distance is exactly what it sounds like! These are just a few options for dogs that like to chase plastic.

Check out skyhoundz.com or hyperflite.com for information on the sport and to get dog-specific discs.

Agility

When people think of dog sports, most people think of agility. Agility is an obstacle course for dogs. They jump over fences, go through tunnels, weave through poles, run up and down an A-frame, and navigate a teeter totter. It's athletic, it's timed, and it's beautiful to see the communication between handlers and their dogs. It takes a lot of work to get the fastest time, and have your dog listen to you while you instruct him through the course. It's such a fantastic way to bond with your dog, teach impulse control, teach confidence, and you learn a ton about off-leash handling skills in this setting.

It is important to do this sport safely. More injuries occur when handlers just drag their dog over a jump, disregard contact points (places on an obstacle that a dog must put their feet on to prevent injury) or put the jump bar too high for a beginner dog. A great instructor will have skid-proof equipment, use shock-absorbing floors, and work with the handler to teach appropriate techniques for sports handling.

*Lyric jumps through a tire jump: a common obstacle on an agility course.
She is owned by Leah Tremble, CPDT-KA of Blue Skies Ahead Training.*

Many reactive or shy dogs can excel in this activity with a skilled instructor. Training centers all over the country are incorporating sports, including agility, to help dogs gain confidence and skills. Even if you elect to never compete in this event, the skills your dog will learn are still invaluable. I recommend this sport to most adolescent dogs that have completed a basic manners or puppy class. You work on the same skills as you would in an advanced manners class, but the adolescent puppies do much better with moving around in the way that only a well-managed sports class will allow.

For more information on agility, go here: http://www.usdaa.com/ or here: https://www.akc.org/events/agility/

Nose Work®/ Tracking / Scenting Games

Did you know that dogs like to sniff things? Yeah, I know, it caught me by surprise, too! If you have a dog that loves nothing more than putting his nose to the ground, this is the activity for you. He's telling you "please, let me sniff SOMETHING!" If you find yourself saying, "No, let's go, stop sniffing that, come on, no!" for the entire walk, why not teach him how to search for things you want him to find? In a good Nose Work® class, you learn how scent travels, what your dog "sees" with his nose, and teach your dog that it's ok to sniff in a particular setting, when searching for a particular thing. It's a ton of fun for your dog. Typically, the act of searching for something specific tires dogs out in a relatively short period of time,

92

because they're using a lot of brain power to accomplish a task. Most people are surprised at how tired their dog is after these classes!

Think of mindlessly flipping through a magazine or reading an incredibly engaging book. Which is more satisfying? If you're flipping through the magazine, you're probably bored and looking for something to bide the time. If you're really taking information out of a book, you're processing that information and are likely more satisfied overall about the reading. The same principle applies to dogs that just sniff everything (biding the time), or have a directive (reading a really engaging book). Plus, this is something you can do in your home once you have the basic skills, and it's really inexpensive. I can't recommend this class enough.

Check out https://performancescentdogs.com/, https://www.nacsw.net/ or http://www.k9nosework.com/ for more information.

Dock Diving

A Belgian Malinois reaches for a bumper over a 20,000 gallon pool
Photo by Eric Kilby of Somerville, Massachusetts

Dock Diving is a sport in which dogs perform versions of long jump, high jump and sprint relays to put it in Track-And-Field terminology. Labradors, spaniels, and other water dogs tend to excel in this sport. If your dog is acclimated to water, your dog is toy driven, and you don't mind the smell of a wet dog, then you might have a contender.

The gist of the sport is simple. A handler will place the dog at the head of a dock. The dog stays at the start line while the handler walks to the end of the dock with the dog's favorite toy. When the handler is ready, the dog is released and takes off at full speed down the dock. The handler throws the toy into the water and the dog leaps for it. When this long jump is done correctly, the dog reaches for the toy while it's in the air, stretching his nose to get it. When the dog hits the water, they mark how far he went. Lather, rinse, repeat.

For the high jump version of the sport, a bumper is placed on a pole arm, above the pool. The dog has to jump vertically to grab the toy. The highest jump wins. If there is a Belgian Malinois in the class, chances are it will take the gold, like the dog in the above photo (he won the event). This is the same breed of dog used in Seal Team Six's mission to capture Osama Bin Laden. These dogs are athletic, and can jump over your high school student without a running start.

Check out http://dockdogs.com/ and http://www.ultimateairdogs.com/eventsexplained.html for more information on this sport!

Flyball

Addie is still flying high in Flyball at age 7.
This beautiful Australian shepherd is owned, trained, and loved by Liz and Dave Strauss of Needham, MA

Flyball is a relay event with four dogs on each team. There are two lanes, each with four jumps, and a box at the end of the runway. One dog from each team is released on their lane when the judge says "go." The dog sprints down the lane, leaps over the jumps, and hits the box, which releases a tennis ball. The dog catches the ball, turns around, and goes back over the four jumps (still carrying the ball). As soon as the first dog crosses the start line, the next dog on the team is released. This pattern continues until all four dogs on each team complete their runs. Since two teams run simultaneously, the faster relay team wins the heat.

Here's the best part: If you have a small, fast dog, you are highly desired! They want you, and they want your dog. The jumps for the entire team are set to the height appropriate for the shortest dog on the team. This means, if you have four German shepherds, the jumps are going to be pretty high and the dogs will have to exert more effort to get over the jumps. If you have three shepherds and a five-pound Chihuahua, the jumps for all the dogs are set to the height appropriate for the Chihuahua. The shepherds won't even have to jump—they can just breeze over the jumps in stride. Even the small guys can do Flyball, and it's absolutely encouraged!

This a team sport, unlike the other sports on this list, so there is a higher level of human socialization at these events, which is an added bonus.

Find a flyball club in your area: http://www.flyball.org/getstarted/

Find out more about flyball: http://flyballdogs.com/

Earthdog™

Many of the terrier breeds love to dig, have high-prey drive, and really want to do what they were bred for- hunting underground vermin. If you have a West Highland terrier, dachshund, Jack Russell terrier, or another small terrier, then Earthdog ™ is for you! This is a timed event with terriers specifically in mind.

There is a system of "underground" tunnels for a dog to run through, in order to locate a caged rat. The rat is totally safe, as it's caged and barricaded off. Some groups elect to use rat scent on a stuffed rat, which works just fine and doesn't stress out a live animal. When a handler is given the "go," the dog is released into the maze and has to find the rat. If the dog gets stuck, the tunnel roof comes off in sections so the dog can be retrieved easily. It's totally safe (as long as your dog can fit in the tunnel) and it really allows for these terrier types to use their instinctual skills.

For more information, check out https://www.akc.org/events/earthdog/ and http://www.earthdog.net/

Additional Ideas:

Most urban environments have a place where you can just get away for a little while. Take your dog hiking, swimming, or teach your dog tricks you can Google. Kyra Sundance has 1,000 tricks that vary from simple to flashy on her YouTube channel, if you want ideas!

Sue Putnam typically leaves the city with her huskies, Kimmi and Winnie, for proper sledding trails. In January, Boston was crippled by three feet of snow, and the roads were shut down for 28 hours. Sue just couldn't resist a bit of a jaunt down Huron Avenue in Cambridge, MA. Her neighbor, George Anderson, snapped this photo, which went viral. George's dog, Pepper, a Havaneese/Shih tsu mix, would not be interested in this activity.

What if my dog isn't active/What if I'm not active?

There are many options for you if either party isn't active! If you can find something that you like to do, and more importantly that your *dog* likes to do, and you can do this activity together, then you are providing a job for your dog. That's what matters.

CGC / Canine Good Citizen Test:

This is the AKC's test to help owners work on basic manners for their dogs. The dog is tested on tasks, such as accepting a friendly stranger, grooming, body handling, staying calm when the owner is absent, and passing by a dog without excitement and lunging. It's the basis for any pet therapy work, AKC obedience, and is a great goal for most handlers who just want to get the basics down pat. There are AKC evaluators in every state who can test you for the Canine Good Citizen exam. Just go to the AKC website (www.akc.org) and look for an evaluator in your area, or join an obedience club that uses positive reinforcement techniques.

Rosie the Leonberger had to earn her Canine Good Citizen before testing for pet therapy certification. This photo was snapped by her proud owner, Stephen Weil.

Pet Therapy:

Pet Partners and Therapy Dogs International are two agencies that certify dogs in the field of pet therapy. The Canine Good Citizen test (see above) is a great place to start, as the first ten requirements for these exams happen to be the same requirements for the CGC. Some organizations require the CGC as well as a pet therapy certification, so check with the organization to see what requirements need to be fulfilled.

Boisterous dogs may need more work and training to be successful, so make sure you are doing therapy work because your dog loves it, not because you really, really, really want a therapy dog. It's better to be honest about the type of work you and your dog are suited for. If you have a laid-back, easygoing dog that adores people, can handle distractions and isn't freaked out by beeping medical equipment, you likely have a great candidate for pet therapy.

When Rose the Border collie isn't herding goats with her owner, Liz Shaw of Magical Mutt Training, she moonlights as a therapy dog. She keeps a busy calendar, and is happier for it.

Rally and Competition Obedience:

Obedience and Rally are fun individual exercises, and both happen to be a great foundation for agility. You can take competition classes and not ever compete, or strive to get several titles on your dog. It's completely up to you and your dog.

I generally encourage students to use Rally Obedience as a starting point because it tends to be less pressure on the handler and you can practice on your own at home. Rally Obedience is a course, like agility, but without the physical obstacles. Instead, Rally focuses on obedience maneuvers. Essentially, the dog and handler follow the instructions on a series of signs on a course, and follow the instructions on each sign. At the novice level, handlers can do the exercises with a leash, but as the team advances, the leash is left behind, and the team competes for the best time on a course. You can print off the signs and practice at home, which is great for training, a nice bonding activity, and fun activity for both parties! Personally, I like the pressure-free way of self-teaching, and the social aspect of doing Rally once a week at a dog training club to stay motivated. Students can just attend classes at an obedience club, or compete in three levels of Rally Obedience, earning titles along the way!

Competition Obedience can include several tasks, ranging from tossing a dumbbell and asking the dog to bring it back, to asking the dog to perform a three minute "stay" with the handler absent from the ring. There are walking patterns, recall exercises, and dozens of exercises that improve training, basic obedience, and attention to the handler—all of these have incredibly useful real-world applications. There are so many things to do in these obedience classes, which only improve a dog's ability to perform everyday tasks in the real world, but in a fun and structured manner.

For information on rally go here: https://www.akc.org/events/rally/getting_started.cfm and for information regarding competition obedience, check here: https://www.akc.org/events/obedience/

Two signs in Rally Obedience, or "Rally-O"

The Most Important Thing You Can Do is simply spend time with your dog doing *something*, preferably something that works on the relationship between you and your dog. Dogs are social creatures, and they depend on us. Many breeds were bred to do a specific job and often that job also required people (herding sheep requires both a dog and a shepherd, for example). Take your dog for a hike, or a walk on the beach. Let him forage for food, or sniff something on your walk. Work on obedience commands. Any time you spend exercising a dog's brain will help your relationship with your pet. If you add physical activity, and give him something he likes to do as an outlet, you'll have a much more satisfied dog, while also ensuring the longevity of your sofa.

The most important thing is to spend time with your dog,
doing something…legal.
(Sarah Rae Easter and her dog, Lila, do not advocate breaking the law.)

Off-Leash Time

Considerations, unleashed!

Previous chapters discussed ways to keep your confined dog happy through structured activities, like classes, and mentally satisfied with the use of puzzle toys. Included in this chapter are the unstructured activities, like off-leash hiking and swimming, as a means of exercise. Should every dog engage freely?

I've learned that the one skill everyone wants in a class is "come when called," another term for "recall." Everything else is viewed as a distant second-tier skill. Most people have the vision of their dog running in a field or the woods, swelling orchestral music in the background, and obediently returning to their calling master. In reality, when left untrained, dogs and owners engage in an age-old game called catch-the-cheeky-dog. While this is great fun for the dog, it's incredibly frustrating for the dog owner. If you want a good laugh, search YouTube for "Jesus Christ in Richmond Park"[15] for the funniest and most frustrating game of catch-the-cheeky-dog I've seen. This might hit too close to home for many of you, but I promise you will still laugh.

"You can take my lands, but you can never take my FREEEEEEEDOOOOOOOM!"
Bourbon just loves running. His owners, Sarah and Olivier, work every day on his recall.
Photo by Nicole Warner

When these happy off-leash dogs charge up to people, or to other dogs passing by on sidewalks, streets, or other shared spaces, things can get dicey. That dog is incredibly friendly, and I can see the enthusiasm on that dog's face, but what about my dog? She isn't so friendly to happy dogs

---

[15] JAGGLL113 "JESUS CHRIST IN RICHMOND PARK: ORIGINAL UPLOAD" https://www.youtube.com/watch?v=3GRSbr0EYYU , November 13, 2011

charging at her, and she has every right to shared space. Who's right? Who's wrong? How can happy dogs enjoy off-leash time, while not getting muddy paw prints on people who don't like dogs? How can happy dogs enjoy off-leash time while not setting off the space-sensitive leashed dogs across the park?

What it's like for the other person when your dog charges to say 'Hi':

Zeppelin, my husband's greyhound, was 80 pounds, and he was the sweetest thing on four feet. Sadie had what we call in this business "trust issues". We let people know as they approached with their dogs that she was not friendly with other dogs. To assuage the unneighborly commentary, we would follow up with how cute their pet was and continue on our walk. Most owners thanked us for mentioning it, and everyone was happy.

One day, I rounded a corner. Both of my dogs were leashed and I saw a woman with her three mini poodles coming out of a door across the street. I assumed that her dogs were leashed, so I brought my attention down to Sadie, had her do some tricks, and kept her attention on me while the woman started her walk. The next thing I knew, she started to yell at her dogs, which brought my attention up, just in time to see the flock of three mini apricot poodles running across a street, dodging a car, and charging at my dogs. She yelled out that they were friendly, and at the same time, I yelled out that mine were not. I held on to Sadie's head collar, as her "friendly" dogs muzzle-punched and bit Sadie under her belly. Sadie did not bite, but I'm pretty sure it's only because I was holding her head.

We do our best as trainers and owners to keep a potentially bad situation at bay. However, sometimes you cannot control for all of the other variables, like the persistent owner who insists, "My dog just wants to say hi!"; or the excited handler who, despite your best efforts, confidently asserts that your dog is too cute to ever hurt another dog; or the woman who can't control her three dogs as they charge across a busy street.

While I'm sure she's a perfectly nice woman and neighbor, she just simply did not understand that her actions were incredibly dangerous to her dogs, drivers, and my dogs. This is why leash laws exist. They aren't to make everything a no-fun zone for your dog, but they exist to give dogs like Sadie space they need, dogs like these poodles a safety net because they can't be trusted to come when called, and drivers the peace of mind they aren't going to hit an off-leash dog on their evening commute.

There is a strong argument that dogs should have a reliable recall, even in parks. Dogs have four legs and people have two. Guess who's going to win in a foot race every time? More importantly consider the following scenario: You have an incredibly friendly, social dog that's racing across a field to say hi to another dog or a kid. Chances are the dog on the other side of the field is a nice dog, but he might not be too keen on your dog's exuberant greeting behavior. As a result, he may react playfully, or he may react with a growl, lunge, fight, or bite. If he's running up to a kid, the kid might be fine with approaching dogs; but consider briefly this was a kid who was attacked by dogs before and is scared. Maybe this is a kid who has never seen a dog, or has allergies. Perhaps it's a kid who is really rough with dogs and could put your dog at risk of injury (intentional or not).

Sarah Grandin is always working on ways to improve Bourbon's ability to come when called. Every single day, Bourbon has to earn his off leash time. If he can't handle off leash time on a particular day, he doesn't get off leash time that particular day. It's a work in progress. Photo by Nicole Warner

Consider for a moment that the previously mentioned leashed dog might be on leash, because it's illegal to be off-leash in most parks and the owner might be a law-abiding citizen. The dog might be on leash because he has canine papilloma (a common virus I affectionately call "puppy herpes," which are very contagious warts). The leashed dog might be on leash because he's not friendly and doesn't appreciate other dogs in his face. The leashed dog might be on leash because his recall isn't so great. The leashed dog may do much better with an approaching *leashed* dog, or one that has a decent recall. The leashed dog might be a recent rescue that is terrified, scared, or not appropriately socialized. Maybe the leashed dog is injured, has arthritis, or just had surgery. You don't know what is

103

going on with the other dog. In an urban environment, it's likely that you encounter these types of dogs every single day, and every day, you are unknowingly contributing to those owners having a more difficult time helping their dogs that need space.

When I teach classes, the friendly dogs come in pulling their owners into the classroom space, eager to see what new adventures are going to happen. All the while, there are dogs in the corner demonstrating, with very clear signals, that they don't like the new dog approaching. Think about some stranger on the train reaching over and giving you a noogie. Now think about how your dog feels when some unfamiliar dog bounds up with no social skills, and doesn't get the hint to back off. Your dog might be the friendliest dog in the whole wide world. The other dog might not be, or just might need some space. Don't assume that it's ok, and don't risk an incident.

Put another way, dogs, like people, can be introverts or extroverts, and like people, this can be dependent on context. My husband is generally soft-spoken, and most would describe him as an introvert, but if you get him around his friends, or watching a football game, he's quite the opposite. Conversely, I tend to be very outgoing and extroverted, except in front of people I highly respect in my field. Then I become uncharacteristically shy, awkward, and nervous. Sadie adored our greyhound and she had one Boston terrier friend. Otherwise, she was not interested in other canine playmates, and who was I to say she had to engage with strange dogs? She had her people, she had her two canine companions, and that was enough for her.

Yes, I really wanted a dog that loved other dogs. I envisioned a life of going to the dog park, and off-leash hiking. I wanted to take her to doggie daycare and drop her off to play with other dog friends while I traveled— but that's not the dog I ended up with. I couldn't make her love other dogs any more than my parents could make me love spiders, but I was able to get her to tolerate living around other dogs within very particular parameters. One of those parameters was that she was afforded just a little bit of space that wasn't infringed upon by other dogs. Even friendly ones. Sadie wasn't, and isn't, the only dog in the city that has an owner working incredibly hard to get just a little bit of space. It's really hard for dog owners, dog lovers, to say, "No, please, stay away!" I find that this is one of the more challenging parts to owning a dog that needs space in a city of friendly dogs. People think they did something wrong because their dog is different and their dog needs space, unlike the other dogs in the fields, parks, and hiking trails. People hate to say, "No—stay away," because as much as the dog needs space, these are dog-loving people who love other dog-loving people. It's hard to turn your back on your tribe.

I found the only thing that worked to give Sadie her personal-space-bubble was to stand my ground and firmly state "Not Friendly!" to every oncoming dog owner. I used to feel terrible for saying it—like I was proclaiming on a mountain top that I had a bad dog, which I emphatically did not. Once I realized that Sadie wasn't alone, and that she was a wonderful dog that happened to need a little space, like thousands of dogs in the Metro-Boston region, I stopped feeling guilty. Wavering, or saying, "She's sort of friendly but doesn't like black dogs, or men with hats..." doesn't work, because if there is any wiggle room, well-intentioned dog owners will take it upon themselves to suggest that their dog is the exception to the rule. To be fair, I live in Boston, and subtlety is not a Boston *thing*. However, the most important factor to her safety was that she had eight feet of space (the length of her leash plus my arm), and that I remained her advocate, always.

Some of these happy, off-leash dogs might just want to enthusiastically say hi to people, many of whom will not appreciate getting leaped on by a dog, no matter how adorable, or how fluffy. Particularly in shared spaces, like community parks and off-leash hiking areas, the onus is on the dog owner to control his or her dog. If that can't be done reliably with vocal commands, then a leash needs to be on the dog until he's otherwise trained.

I don't let my two-year-old daughter out of my sight, not because I don't want her to have a good time, but because she's two. She does not have the appropriate skill set to engage appropriately with strangers. She is a two-year-old who is unable to avoid trouble wherever it happens to be. Additionally, not every person loves kids and even the most kid-crazy adults certainly wouldn't appreciate her peanut-butter crusted fingers crawling all over them. I think she's adorable, but I'm her mom. I'm supposed to think she's cute. Not everyone appreciates her, and not everyone appreciates your dog jumping up to say hi. Guess what? That is totally, completely, and perfectly ok.

Cider Doughnut of Somerville.
Your intention to love her isn't permission to come into her space.
Owner Alison MacDonald purchased this particular leash slider on Etsy to advocate for her canine partner. There are great resources for dogs like Sadie and Cider.

If your dog eventually earns the privilege of going off-leash, which isn't a given, you still have to keep up on training. Just like my kid loses out on opportunities when she messes up, our dogs need to go back on leash if they make a mistake, and more training can be applied. Some dogs should never be released from their leashes unless in a fenced-in area, and again—that's totally and completely fine. Your dog isn't a bad dog because it can't resist the thrill of the chase in an open field. Freedom is a privilege, not a right, and in a city, it's better to be safe than sorry.

I'm positive I didn't make any friends that day I told Poodle-Lady that her dogs really needed to be leashed, and that if my dog had bitten hers, she would be responsible because of existing leash laws. When she continued to insist that she was only getting them outside to the back yard and that it's no big deal, I told her it clearly was, considering they ran away from her into danger. At the very least, they should be under voice control, because it could be something else, perhaps a teenager behind the wheel of an oncoming car, a school bus, or a person who couldn't control his reactive dogs, which would have ended up significantly worse for her tiny, bite-sized poodles.

Just because my dog didn't bite hers on that day, does not mean it couldn't happen. Sadie had bitten before, which is why I was really careful and honest to passing dog handlers by saying "not friendly" when dogs looked like they were approaching. At the end of the day, I was Sadie's advocate, but I was looking out for the safety of the other dogs in my community as well. It really doesn't matter if you're walking 20 feet to your backyard, or two miles around a public park. If your dog cannot come back, reliably, in the face of all the possible distractions in a nutty, urban environment, your dog must be leashed in the city. Period. There are just too many things that can go wrong, and too many variables to account for that are completely out of your control.

Rule #1 of dog training: Your dog might be the friendliest dog in the world, but that doesn't mean every other dog wants to be friends (and that's ok).

Rule #2 of dog training: Your dog needs a solid recall, if he's off-leash.

Pippin will ALWAYS come for a tennis ball, especially if his photographer mom, Suzanne Hunt, is holding the flinging arm!

There are many ways to work on recall. This book isn't a how-to, but instead, outlines things to consider when you have a dog in the city. You can take a class, join a dog club, or practice sound scientific techniques that you can watch on YouTube (Victoria Stilwell, Sophia Yin, Kikopup and

Zak George have excellent resources on teaching a dog to "come"). Every basic manners class should dedicate time to recall, while also addressing other basic skills such as sit, down, stay, and, good-God-don't-eat-that! Some classes are even designed specifically for working on one thing only: Teach your dog to come when called.

There is one other way to work recalls and off-leash skills: canine sports. In most dog sports the dog has to be able to execute skills, such as "go this way," "do this thing," "come" and "stay" while off leash. These dogs are able to run, jump, and play, but also have excellent impulse control skills, which are something all dogs, not just dogs in the city, need to have programmed. Sports are a great way to teach the dog that you are more exciting than those other exciting things in the environment, which doesn't come naturally. It takes a lot of work.

My Dog Doesn't Need A Leash:

We have two neighbors who walk their dogs without leashes. One dog is a rather large mix that stays at his owners heels, and as far as I can tell, they have never had an incident. The other is a Chihuahua I watched almost get hit by a car on two separate occasions, when it darted out to see someone across the street. One of these dogs clearly should be walked on a leash, but I would argue that both should be leashed.

When I was new to the city, I would take Sadie down the street to a doggie play group in the park after work. We'd see the same friendly dogs and familiar faces. One of these dogs was Shred, a medium-sized black mop of a dog. Shred was never more than a couple of feet behind his owner, and his owner never used a leash. He didn't have to, because Shred was always two strides behind him. One day, they were crossing McGrath Highway on their way home from the dog park. They had the right of way, but there was a minivan that ran a red light. The driver of the van gunned the engine to make it through the intersection, ignoring the pedestrians in the crosswalk. Shred's owner ran forward to avoid the car, but Shred didn't. Had he been leashed, the owners' forward motion would have at least pulled Shred enough to maybe miss the oncoming van. I'm not going so far as to say that if Shred had been on leash that he would have been ok, but I will say there is a chance this would have been a near miss instead of a direct hit. If it were my dog, that's a chance I'd happily take every day of the week.

Many people want their dogs to be great off-leash walking companions, and I will admit that it looks impressive when a dog is dutifully following behind his owner without a leash. I don't advise this practice for a variety of reasons. There is the unforeseen variable (like Shred), or something particularly exciting across the street (as in the case of the Chihuahua). Dogs are animals, and animals have a mind of their own, even if they are impeccably trained. I like having the safety net, and hopefully I'll never, ever need it.

"I can hit 40 mph in two strides. Can you?"
Photo by Tammi Searle of her greyhound, Missy

A dog should be able to run, play, and unapologetically roll in goose poop. However, like with most things, certain conditions must be met before those activities should be allowed. Your dog should be allowed freedom in the city if all the following conditions are met:

- It's never ok to allow your dog to charge other people, or other dogs as a greeting. Etiquette works for people and for dogs.

- Your dog is under voice control 100% of the time. One command, one action. "Sadie, come!" The following is not considered a reliable recall, or anything remotely similar to voice control: "Please, Sadie, come! I said come—NO! COME! SADIE—&#!$? Come here NOW! It's OK! She's friendly!"

- If your dog is not under voice control, use a 30' long line to work recall with your dog. Get into a recall class, attend a free recall clinic if they are available in your city, or watch a few YouTube videos

109

from Victoria Stilwell or another certified dog trainer. Get into a sport like disc or agility where your dog is allowed to run, jump, play, and go full tilt, but you can stop the dog with your voice, and your dog learns attention in a fun way.

- You are in a dog-appropriate place in your city, not on the sidewalk or in a little-kid tot-lot. Too many things can go wrong on the sidewalks, and dog urine in a kid's playground is really gross. Local parks and hiking trails where dogs are permitted off-leash, dog friendly beaches, fenced-in dog parks, etc. are appropriate off-leash outlets for your urban dog, but only if your dog can handle those situations.

- Some dogs, like sight hounds, generally should never be let off-leash in an unfenced area. The greyhound rescue group we used stated on their website that they do not recommend letting these dogs off leash at all. We never let Zeppelin off his leash unless in a fenced-in area. Given his speed and disinclination for coming back, I understand why. When a dog hits 40 miles-per-hour in two strides, they can get really far, really fast. Seek out safe, fenced-in places for your *friendly* dog to run. Keep in mind, as mentioned in a previous chapter, that not all dogs will do ok in a dog park. If your dog is sometimes ok with large groups, and not at others, don't take your dog to a dog park. Work with a trainer to figure out where your dog can get appropriate exercise without putting other dogs at risk, or stressing your dog out unnecessarily.

- You are paying attention to your dog's behavior and your surroundings. If your dog is off playing with other dogs, you should not be on your cell phone, doing a crossword puzzle, or chatting with other people while ignoring where your dog is. You might want to pay attention to what he's rolling in, if he's chasing a bike, chasing a dog, chasing a squirrel, what he's eating, or where he is pooping. In the city, it's still your responsibility to clean up after your dog, even if your New York Times puzzle is too distracting. Off-leash time is not the time for you to mentally check out; in fact you should be paying more attention to your dog when he's not tethered to you. Wait until your dog is exercised, then go home, have a glass of wine, and tune out the world, or talk to your friend on the phone.

Summary:

Your dog might be excited to say hi to every dog and person he meets, but the other dog might be aggressive, shy, recovering from injury, old, or reactive. Other people might not enjoy your dog's enthusiastic jumps, might be allergic, or have been attacked by dogs in the past. If your dog is friendly, find appropriate places to unleash your hound, but only if you have reliable recall. If your dog isn't friendly and needs to run, get a trainer, and get into disc, agility, or other sports so you can learn how to control your dog's impulses while still getting exercise. Lastly, never, ever assume that the other dog is friendly and ok with greetings from strange dogs. In the city, chances are high that the other dog might not be social, and that's totally ok.

Gouda is a 4-year-old adora-mutt from a North Carolina rescue.
She now resides in Metro-Boston with the Steiman family.
She's playing outside at a local park, working on recall, with a leash on.

Trainers, Consultants & Behaviorists

What professional do I need for my dog?

Most questions I get as a dog trainer fall into one of two categories.

1. "Can you just train my dog to do something?" This can be sit, stay, fetch a beer, or roll over. It can also include walk nicely on a leash, play competitive disc, or earn a Canine Good Citizen title.
2. "Can you train my dog NOT to do something?" This tends to encompass stop barking, stop jumping, stop eating shoes, stop eating chairs, stop eating rocks, stop peeing on other dogs, and other such behaviors that dog owners find irritating, harmful, annoying or in the case of humpers, embarrassing.

Ideally, we dog trainers don't just teach dogs *not to do something,* but instead teach alternative behaviors. Dogs tend to learn to DO something much better than they learn to NOT do something, so if we are teaching an alternative behavior to the barking, jumping, or humping we are going to be much more successful.

I can teach a dog to do something after assessing the following:

- What is the desired behavior? Is it something most dogs can actually do? I can teach a dog to roll over, but to do your taxes? Probably not.
- Does the dog have health issues that hinder movement, preventing this behavior? Teaching a dog with arthritis to roll over might not be the best idea.
- What is the personality of the dog? Does this behavior affect the comfort of the dog? If a dog is scared of other dogs, but the owner wants the dog to play at the dog park, we have an emotional state incompatible with a desired behavior. This will take a lot of work, and might not be something that's in the best interest of the nervous dog.
- What foundational skills does the dog already have? If the dog doesn't know how to sit, but the owner wants a dog to stop jumping on people, there is much more work involved.
- What is the emotional state of the dog at the time of our meeting? Is the dog happy and a fast learner? Is the dog shut down or nervous?

There might be occasions during the course of an evaluation or phone consultation that a client is referred to a behavior consultant or an applied animal behaviorist instead of a dog trainer. A veterinarian might recommend a trainer for some behaviors and recommend a veterinary behaviorist for others. The guy at the dog park might suggest that someone seek out the assistance of a *behavioralist*, which is unfortunate because there is no such thing as a *behavioralist* in the dog world. That term is reserved for political science folk. While I'm sure they are intelligent specialists, the behavioralist movement does not lend itself particularly well to dog training or behavior. Unless the behavioralist is also a certified dog professional, he or she might not have the expertise to help a dog behave.

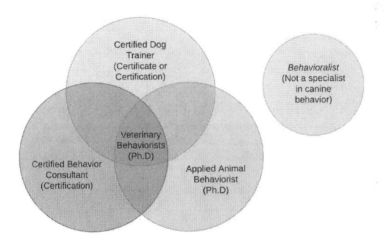

It can be challenging and frustrating to figure out what professional is best suited for a particular behavior, especially considering that there is quite a bit of overlap among these specialists. This breakdown will help explain what each professional does and how to find a reliable one in your area.

Dog Trainer
Some Affiliated Certifications and Certificates - Certification Council of Pet Dog Trainers (CPDT-KA and CPDT-KSA); San Francisco Dog Training Academy (CTC); International Association of Dog Training Professionals

(PTDI); Karen Pryor Academy (KPA); Animal Behavior College (ABC)

What trainers do:

Trainers are the teachers of the animal world, and the way each individual teaches can vary greatly. Trainers can teach group classes that focus on the basics such as sit, down, stay, or come when called; they can conduct individual or private training in your home (home school!); and they can teach sports, such as agility, canine disc or competition obedience. They also can focus on rally, dock diving, and other activities in the form of a club, class, or organization. These professionals are the ones to go to for manners-related issues, so if you have a door dasher or a counter surfer, you might call a trainer. If you have a dog that is reactive on walks, if you are preparing for a new baby, or require puppy basics, a trainer is likely the right specialist for you.

Where they overlap with other specialists:

Trainers can teach tricks, manners, and sports, but dog trainers also work to affect emotion and behavior, which is the focus of the other professions noted in this chapter. When a dog is exhibiting "bad behavior," it can be indicative that he is having an acute emotional response to leash walks, is physically distressed when left alone, or it could mean that he just needs more exercise. Many trainers can help with mild-to-moderate cases of separation anxiety, leash reactivity, mild-to-moderate fear of strangers, and some cases of non-generalized aggression. Some trainers are qualified to handle aggression and more significant behavior problems, but make sure you get references for these trainers. In such cases, make sure they are certified through a reputable organization, are properly insured, and aren't using intimidation and fear-based dog training techniques, which science has proven to exacerbate problem behaviors, particularly in an urban environment.

It's on you to do your research. Does the trainer have a reputable certification in which their skills were assessed by taking a test? How long has the trainer been working in the industry? Does that certification need to be maintained with continuing education credits? Does the trainer's business practice line up with the code of ethics set forth by the certifying body? In other words, does the trainer have a positive reinforcement certification, but is using shock collars and alpha rolls? If there are glaring discrepancies between the standards of the certification and the practices of the trainer, you might want to find another trainer.

Is the trainer a certified trainer for *pet dogs*? In our area, there are many former police-dog trainers who are branching out and working on pet dogs. Though I have immense respect for the boys in blue (I'm the daughter of a police officer), the dogs they train need to find criminals or take down a human being who is pointing a gun in their face. These trainers are fantastic at what they are certified in: finding dogs that are genetically able to go into intense, chaotic situations and bring bad-guys to justice. Most Australian labradoodles I know will never have to meet a drug lord, find accelerant for an arson case, or take down a criminal on the lam. Unless the trainer also has a certification in *pet* dog training (or is working towards certification), consider hiring another trainer for your family pet. Hire the police-dog trainer if you're looking to join The Force, or want to have a demonstration in canine takedowns at a local event.

Does the trainer have a certificate that states the instructor successfully completed a course? How long was the course and is there a test at the end? Keep in mind that not all certifications and certificates are created equally, so make sure you do your homework. Training certificates are handy additions to certifications. Certificates are also a wonderful "in" for the basics or a specific area of training (like clicker-training or pet first-aid). Some certificate programs are actually incredibly thorough and more intense than certifications, but some others are not as reputable. Initials alone do not make a trainer.

Kaiju the Shiba inu attends a puppy class with five other puppies. Here he is working on an important city-skill: attention! Photo by Nobuko Ichikawa

In general, a certification indicates knowledge gained over a period of time, by apprenticing, calculating hours, skill assessment and lots of studying for an exam given by a third party, like the Council of Certified Pet Dog Trainers (CCPDT). A certificate, however, indicates that someone was able to take a weekend course, or longer, and the degree of the knowledge gained is assessed by the group issuing the certificate. Some are great, like KPA and the SPCA (which take months to complete and are very thorough), while others are good résumé padders and are great indicators of continuing education. Make sure you know the credentials, and what the trainer had to do to earn those credentials before hiring.

Where a trainer would not be appropriate:

Trainers are not veterinarians. Though trainers can suspect underlying medical conditions as they relate to behavior, and they might even guess correctly what the problem is, they do not have the medical expertise to diagnose medical conditions in any animal, and they have no business diagnosing *any* medical condition. A good trainer will say "This looks wrong. Go see your vet."

If a dog shuts down in a classroom setting or breaks his teeth on the bars of his crate due to severe separation anxiety, and the only way to help the animal is to work on emotional response, a behavior consultant, applied animal behaviorist, or veterinary behaviorist might be more appropriate. Of course, this depends on the degree of the problem behavior and the qualifications of the consulting trainer.

When you should consider calling a trainer:
- Classroom work (puppy class, basic manners class, agility class)
- Door dashing
- "Manners" issues, like jumping behaviors, or impulse control issues
- Sports and activities
- Mild to moderate reactivity to dogs or other people
- Mild to moderate fear issues
- Referred to by a behavior consultant or a veterinary behaviorist

Behavior Consultants and Applied Animal Behaviorists:
Some Affiliated Reliable Certifications - Animal Behavior Society (ACAAB & CAAB); International Association of Animal Behavior Consultants (CABC & CDBC); International Association for the Study of Animal Behavior (CCAB); Certification Council for Professional Dog Trainers (CBCC-KA)

What do behavior consultants and applied animal behaviorists do?

Behavior consultants and applied animal behaviorists have an interest in why animals do what they do, and more specifically, why a behavior goes awry. They are the psychological rehabilitators of the animal world. If a dog is having an acute emotional response to the mailman, aggresses at people, has a bite history, has moderate-severe separation anxiety, or seems to be having a difficult time emotionally with one (or more) parts of daily life, then one of these professionals might be the way to go.

What does the term "behaviorist" actually mean?

Is the guy down the street a behaviorist? If he's putting prong collars on dogs and hasn't taken a single class in animal behavior, chances are high that he isn't a behaviorist. In our region we have several "professionals" who use choke chains, prong collars, alpha-roll dogs and ask for submission while calling themselves behaviorists. This is (in my opinion) unethical and incorrect terminology.

While there is no governing body as to who can use the term *behaviorist*, the general consensus among professionals is that this term is reserved for those with a doctorate in a related field (such as zoology or biology). These *applied animal behaviorists* have a PhD and are highly qualified to address behavior related issues. Because of their specialty, their expertise, and the fact that these professionals are few, the cost tends to be higher than for a behavior consultant or dog trainer. That being said, if the problem is significant, then this is perhaps the best bet for getting help. Consult with reputable sources, and just like everything else, do your homework before hiring a professional.

In addition to applied animal behaviorists, there are reputable behavior specialists working with challenging behaviors, who don't have a doctorate degree, and are still highly qualified to assist with particularly challenging issues. These professionals, if they have the proper certifications and credentials, call themselves *behavior consultants*.

Where they overlap with other specialists:

Behavior consultants and applied animal behaviorists are the bridge between the veterinary behaviorists and the trainers, in that they use their training background to affect emotionally linked behaviors in troubled dogs, build confidence, or teach dogs behaviors that are incompatible with the problem behavior that they are exhibiting. They also work very closely with veterinary behavior specialists. As a result they tend to have a working knowledge of medical conditions that can produce, or exacerbate, certain behaviors.

A dog may act aggressively for behavioral or medical reasons, or a combination of both. A good behavior consultant or behaviorist would work closely with the client and with the veterinarian to order medical tests that might give some insight into behavior problems. They will use training and medical tools in order to help the animal cope. Not all behavior is medically related, but a good behavior specialist will be able to recognize certain red flags, which may be indicative that there is more to the behavior than meets the eye.

Again, it's critical to note that these professionals are not veterinarians, so they are not able to diagnose a condition in a pet; however, they have a working knowledge of problem behaviors and how they might relate medically, so they can work with your vet to make sure you are getting the best possible care. While applied animal behaviorists have a doctorate, unless they are veterinarians as well, they shouldn't be diagnosing medical conditions. They are certainly qualified to talk with your vet candidly about what was observed in the consultation, which might lead to a quicker diagnosis if medical issues are suspected.

Where a behavior consultant /applied animal behaviorist would not be appropriate:
Though these professionals work closely with veterinarians and veterinary behaviorists, they cannot diagnose medical conditions, nor can they prescribe medicine to your pet unless they also have a medical degree.

When you should contact a behavior specialist:
- Mild to severe cases of separation anxiety
- Mild to severe cases of leash aggression
- If you suspect there might be a link between health and behavior, a behavior specialist can be a good place to start after you see your veterinarian for a full check-up
- Any dog with an existing bite history, or if you suspect your dog will bite
- Emotional or anxiety disorders; behaviors driven by intense fear or anxiety in your dog (shaking in the bathtub during a thunderstorm, or an inability to cope with new environments)
- Referred to by a veterinary behaviorist, a veterinarian, or a trainer
- Multiple anxieties or problem behaviors (significant fear of loud noises and leash aggression, for example)

Veterinary Behaviorist:
Associated Certification (there is only one):
Diplomate of the American College of Veterinary Behaviorists (DACVB)

What they do:

These specialists are veterinarians who have studied animal behavior. These are medical practitioners who walk the line between the medical world, the behavior world, and the training world. They are appropriate for cases spanning the highly unusual, the most intense forms of aggression or reactivity, or any behavior that has a medical, or suspected medical, component. These veterinarians are board certified diplomates of the American College of Veterinary Behaviorists. They are able to give medications to aid in training and health.

Where they overlap with other specialists:

Veterinary behaviorists have an interest in behavior problems, like the behavior specialists, and they use training techniques to modify behavior, like the trainer. They have the added benefit of a medical degree so they can most directly treat and diagnose physical issues as they relate to behavior. Veterinary behaviorists don't always use medication to treat behavior problems, but they are the most qualified to see the links between behavior, nutrition and health, and can prescribe medication if necessary. They are often the ones requested when a behavior is really out of the ordinary, medical issues are suspected, or as a last ditch effort before sadder, more drastic measures are taken.

Veterinary behavior specialists are also commonly known as "the guys who deal with OCD". If you have a dog that has a behavior that is extreme in some way, such as licks his leg to the point of bleeding or compulsion; chases light or shadows; chases his tail compulsively and can't be distracted; behaviors that look cute at first, but are extremely problematic in real life, there is help.

As of writing this, there are only about 60 veterinary behavior specialists in the United States. If you are not lucky enough to live near a specialist, some partake in a Vet Fax program, where your vet will work with a behavior specialist in your region, to get you the help you require. As a result of being a rare bird, and a very specialized niche, vet behavior specialists are not cheap—but if you have a real problem behavior, or this is your last chance to make things work, their experience is invaluable.

Where a veterinary behaviorist would not be appropriate:
- If you have a dog that is exuberantly jumping up on you at home, or you have a dog that needs a puppy class, see a trainer.
- If you need help with recalling your dog in distracting situations, call a

trainer.
- If you need help with a leash aggressive dog that isn't globally fearful, talk with a trainer or a behavior specialist first.

When you should consider calling a veterinary behaviorist:
- Compulsive disorders, or suspected compulsive disorders, that can cause harm to the animal or others. These behaviors are intense, repetitive, and they cannot be redirected. Compulsive spinning for hours at a time; snapping at invisible flies; constant licking of either the front leg or the hindquarters to the point of bleeding should be reported to your veterinarian.
- Behaviors that are extreme or excessive: If the dog suffers from severe separation anxiety, where he is causing himself physical harm due to anxiety, or if the dog is unable to function with another dog more than 20 feet away.
- If you've ever said this about your dog: "The behavior was sudden, and went away as if nothing happened, like a light switch."
- Behaviors that are likely related to health or a medical condition.
- Dogs that have a significant bite in their history; multiple bites to people or dogs; or "He bit out of nowhere."
- If the behavior isn't getting better with a qualified trainer, consultant, or applied behaviorist, and this is the last possible avenue before euthanasia.
- Referred to by a trainer, your veterinarian, applied animal behaviorist, or a behavior consultant.

When in doubt, you can always start with any of these professionals on the phone, describe the behavior, and ask if you are contacting the right person. If not, you will be redirected to the appropriate practitioner, if you are starting with a reputable and ethical professional from the get-go. Always look for certifications that you can investigate on your own. For example, if someone is CPDT certified, go to the CPDT website and see what exactly that certification means, how it was obtained, and what the philosophies are of that certifying group. Then, check the website of the professional and make sure that their practices line up with the philosophies of the certifying body.

If you need help finding a trainer, check out http://www.ccpdt.org/ , http://www.apdt.com/ , or https://www.karenpryoracademy.com/ to get started.

If you need help finding a behavior specialist, check out https://iaabc.org/ , http://ccpdt.org, or http://animalbehavior.org to see which professionals are local and reputable.

If you need help finding a board certified veterinary behaviorist, check out www.dacvb.org

If anyone is calling himself a behaviorist and does not have certifications to back up that claim (or has certifications that aren't reliable), than you would do best to look elsewhere for a reputable professional.

Pugs, Not Drugs?

Behavior modification and our dogs.
A love story, with caveats

Had you asked me a decade ago what I thought of behavior modification medication, like "Puppy Prozac" and other such means of drugging a dog to get a better behaved pet, I would have said something to this effect:

"Dogs give up a lot to live in a human environment and we don't give them the outlets they require to survive in a home environment, especially in the city. We come home, walk the dog, and often that isn't enough. Your dog needs more training and exercise. Try agility to channel the energy in a positive way."

My feeling was summed up essentially as 'Pugs, Not Drugs.'

While the above statement is still true, it turns out there is a lot more complexity to the medication issue. Behavior drugs for pets are just as much a hot-button topic as they are for humans… who knew?

Thanks to my personal relationship with a dog that eventually needed behavior modification medication and the respected professionals in the training and medical fields I've been able to work with closely for over a decade, my tune has changed drastically on the subject. I started noticing tangible differences in dogs that just weren't getting enough exercise and dogs that were having a visceral reaction to stimuli in a very real way.

What's Going On?

I can't speak for the country as a whole, but in Massachusetts we are seeing an increase in medication and holistic remedies prescribed for behavior issues. Generally, veterinarians are not prescribing medications willy nilly, but many of the dogs that are trucked, flown, or imported (not just rescues—dogs flown in from breeders, too!) are unable to cope emotionally and physically in a city environment. Although owners love their dogs, love and training might not be enough to help these dogs cope. These dogs can be terrified of all the new experiences they are dealing with (everything from traffic to dishwashers) and they struggle to make it in the big city. Some of these dogs just weren't socialized adequately despite the owner's best intentions, and some of these dogs just don't have a city personality. In many cases, the dogs have significant noise phobias to thunderstorms, which might also generalize to sudden exterior noises, construction, washing machines, fireworks, loud music, garbage trucks and cars honking. Luckily, none of that goes on in a city. Oh wait...uh oh.

Rescue dogs aren't the only dogs that are medicated. Dogs that were bred for very particular jobs but are essentially unemployed can have an exceptionally difficult time, regardless of where they live. Dogs that are bred to be territorial protectors might have difficulty with pedestrians (or as they see it, "trespassers") on the street. It's unfair to ignore instinctual drives and not provide activities that satisfy a dog's genetic programming. These dogs can struggle in urban environments if genetics are ignored.

A Cane Corso (Italian mastiff) is a stunning dog, but taking into consideration its lines, its breeding, its purpose, and putting that dog in an apartment building without any outlets could be a recipe for potential problems, if proper precautions and training protocols are ignored. That same dog that competes in pulling trials, participates in obedience training at a club, is well socialized, and is able to get out of the city from time to time, might do really well. Potential dog owners need to do their homework, lest they end up with a dog that is a mismatch for the family and the environment.

For many dogs, sports, agility, more training and mental stimulation may be the answer. But, when all of those options fail, when there are wacky blood work numbers, when there are significant phobias and anxieties, when nothing else has worked, behavior modification medication in tandem with a behavior plan can be a light on the horizon for those dogs and their owners.

Medicating a dog is a delicate topic, and should be broached with your vet as well as your trainer or behavior specialist. Some people don't want to use behavior modification medications, period, even if doing so would make their dogs happier and able to function better through thunderstorms, generalized anxiety, reactivity, and other problem behaviors that do not go away on their own. These behaviors tend to escalate over time when left untreated. As a dog remains in a prolonged state of stress, physical symptoms may start to appear as well as other behavior breakdowns. If a dog is tense from stress every minute of every day, cortisol (stress hormone) levels increase, which can lead to other physical issues and can decrease the life expectancy of that dog.

We have all experienced short and long-term stress. We feel better once relief is in sight, but might be short tempered when we've experienced a lot of stress for a long period of time. Our backs hurt. Our shoulders tense up and get knotted. We snap at loved ones or strangers. Our dogs are also prone to experiencing a shorter fuse and a slew of physical symptoms when constantly exposed to stress over a time. We owe it to them to help find relief.

On the flip side, some people are too quick to ask for medications, which is why this has become such a hot button topic. There are dogs out there that never get beyond the backyard, never get walked, lunge at people passing by, and are really frustrated by lack of exercise and mental stimulation. Instead of trying to fix the root of the problem with training and exercise, some owners look to drugs for a quick fix. Dogs that have a sudden break down of behavior might need more exercise, or they might have a significant health issue—blindness, arthritis, a sore tooth, sore knees, hearing loss, or thyroid problems. It's absolutely imperative that the very first step you take when your dog is exhibiting a wayward behavior is to see your veterinarian. If the first step from your trainer or behavior consultant does not include a visit with a veterinarian, get a new trainer.

Sadie's Story

In the interest of full disclosure, Sadie was the first dog I owned as an adult, and I made a lot of mistakes with her.

I rescued her from the Franklin County Animal Shelter in Columbus, Ohio, just a couple of weeks after graduating from college. She was a relatively happy dog when we moved to Boston in 2004. She did better in the country, but she managed just fine in the city. We were competing with the Yankee Flyers Dog and Disc Club until 2007. As part of that, she was getting several hours of exercise a night in local baseball parks under the cover of darkness since it was illegal to let dogs run in baseball parks. She went to work with me every day, and life was great for Sadie.

Somewhere around the age of three, Sadie became extremely sensitive to noise. She would violently shake at the sound of construction, thunder and fireworks. Garbage trucks would set her off. Nothing could distract her. She had one of these panic attacks while I was working at the animal hospital, so one of the veterinarians checked her out. Her heart rate was through the roof. She was having a very real, very physical reaction to the construction down the street.

On my second date with my now husband in 2007, I got a phone call from my roommate, who brought Sadie to a 4th of July party in the city. He thought she'd help him with the ladies. He said he was sorry, but that I had to come back to help Sadie. She was hiding in a closet, having buried herself under some dirty laundry, and my roommate was unable to coax her out. The neighbors were setting off fireworks in front of the apartment, and Sadie was absolutely terrified.

There is nothing sadder than seeing your dog shaking, panting, and hiding from something and not being able to do anything to let her know it's ok. It became worse when she turned her nose up at a marinated steak I used to try to coax her out of the closet (since I'm a vegetarian she didn't get meat very often). I had to go into the closet, carry my 40 pound dog past all of her favorite people, and drive her somewhere quiet to find relief.

As time went on, Sadie's phobias got worse, as they tend to do, even with more exercise and mental stimulation. Everything would set her off. The doorbell, trucks pulling up, and finally, she started to develop separation anxiety. Every time we'd leave, she'd panic. She lost her playful demeanor and became an anxious ball of fear and fluff. She was nearly eight years old at the onset of these new clinical anxieties, though they had been building over time.

I thought it was because her exercise regimen had changed, mostly because her physical needs had changed. As an older dog, she tired more quickly, started limping with arthritis and had a heart murmur that needed to be monitored. To work around it, we played ball at the end of our street a few times a day, enjoyed several short walks and had opportunities to get short bursts of aerobic exercise a day. We also used puzzle toys to keep her mentally stimulated. We changed her food to make sure she didn't have too much junk, too much protein, and too much... period.

Our landlord told us that the dogs would bark at the kids in the street after we'd leave for the day. We immediately started putting them upstairs with a gate so they'd have free reign but no visual access to the activity on the street. One day, we got a call from our landlord saying that the dogs were going nuts and that we had to fix it, soon. I asked how long they had been barking, thinking it had just been for the hour I was gone. He said it had been going on for months. MONTHS!? We had no clue it was that bad. Our landlord never told us the behavior was still happening, even after we implored that she kept us in the loop, so we could actively address behaviors at the onset. I sat outside that day, listening to the utter panic in Sadie's barks. I felt horrible.

I missed my old dog, my companion, my buddy. She was in there somewhere, but we really were at a loss. We had talked about drugs as a last resort, but we still wanted to try some other things first. To be perfectly frank, I had even said to my husband "What happens when she bites our greyhound, or attacks our cats? We'd have no recourse but to put her down." I had been thinking it for a while and could only bring it up after having a few glasses of wine one night, because otherwise it was just something I couldn't say out loud. I'm being totally and completely honest. I brought up the discussion of putting my beloved friend to sleep because I've been in this industry long enough to know that putting a nine-year-old dog with a bite history up for adoption does not lead to happily-ever-after. Yet, allowing her to live with such stress and anxiety while putting the other three animals at risk was not fair to her, or the other animals in our home. Things were getting pretty bad.

We knew we had to do something, but every technique we tried left us where we started. We tried a fitted anti-anxiety wrap for storms, which didn't really help her. We tried holistic approaches which have helped some of my students, but the only benefit was that our house smelled like lavender. We tried the ace bandage wrap technique and she just looked silly. We tried counterconditioning the doorbell, which left her anxious and waiting for the doorbell to ring. We tried much more exercise, which didn't help because the root of her problem was anxiety, not lack of exercise. The only thing that got better was walking the dogs, but that meant crossing a busy street and lots of attention training, but Sadie still couldn't relax. Finally, Zeppy picked up on Sadie's anxiety. She would not bark at the passing dog, but Zeppy, sensing her anxiety, would bark, and he barked loudly.

Fan-bloody-tastic.

The final straw was when she lunged at Zeppy for no identifiable reason. Later that same day she jumped a gate I had put upstairs to confine them, so I could go to work. The gate was blocking a stairway, so when she jumped the gate, she fell down the flight of stairs. My landlord called saying there was a loud noise and lots of barking. I got home to see Sadie shaking and whining at the bottom of the stairwell. I immediately called my friend Sip (who happened to be Sadie's vet).

The drug names aren't important, but we tried a couple different ones to find what would help her best. The first one just made her really sleepy and didn't touch the anxiety, though "stoned Sadie" was quite amusing. We tried a second drug, a more permanent solution, and I have to say that it was awesome to have my friend back.

The first 30 days of the medication demonstrated precisely what behavior drugs are supposed to do. She still got nervous during thunderstorms, but snapped out of it in a matter of minutes instead of hours. The doorbell would ring and she would go to her bed, instead of barking and shaking at the door. She would still bark but was eventually able to settle with much more ease. She even tried to play with our greyhound, which was something she didn't do in the three years we had him prior to the medication. The cats started coming out more often. I didn't even realize that they were affected until after Sadie's drugs kicked in.

Perhaps the most brilliant part was that we could pass by dogs on the street without barking or frustration. We still had to work a lot of attention behaviors, and we didn't let her say hi to passing dogs (space was still critical for her success), but to pass a dog eight feet away was a huge milestone for her. As she calmed down passing other dogs, Zeppy calmed down, too. All three of us were able to walk by a dog on the street with a slack leash. She was nine years old when we started this. I thought back, and the last time I could do that with confidence was five years prior.

I was finally able to do the training necessary for Sadie's success, the training that I was previously unable to do because we had hit a wall. We were unable to train the good behaviors in this case, not because of lack of exercise or failure in training techniques, but because her anxiety was so significant that no training would stick. In 2014, she took the Canine Good Citizen test and earned her CGC, just six weeks before she died. One of the requirements of the test is passing by a dog without reacting in any way, which she was able to do with hard work, trust in her handler, training and her happy-pills. No one can take that away from her.

Had I just given her the drugs and not worked on any counterconditioning, or failed to maintain her exercise regimen, the medication would not have worked. She may have been less anxious at first, but the behaviors we disliked would have still been ingrained. She wouldn't know what to do when the doorbell rang, so she likely would still run, charge and bark at the door. With the medication, she still barked at the door, but we were able to send her to the kitchen. Teaching her an alternate behavior when she was anxious was something we weren't able to effectively train for years.

Sadie was back. She was back to being Sadie, a dog that was kind of a bitch from time to time, but a playful, engaging animal that was smarter than our toddler in so many respects. Overall, I felt much better, as did she. It's a choice that isn't right for every dog or every situation, but is a choice I would absolutely make again for her.

When to Consider Behavior Modification Medication:
This absolutely must be a discussion between you, your vet, and your trainer. Everyone needs to be on the same page. There are certain

behaviors that do well with medication in tandem with dog training, and only a certified dog trainer or certified behavior specialist, alongside a vet, should be giving that advice. These professionals need to be using positive techniques. Aversive techniques have been proven scientifically to exacerbate phobias and fears. In short, a prong collar on my neck won't make me any less afraid of spiders. Instead, I'll likely get more stressed, because there are spiders, and also pain if I react inappropriately. The same learning theory that is applicable to humans is applicable to dogs. Be sure you are working with someone skilled, certified, and patient. Make sure that you're prepared for a long road and a lifetime of behavior management. A magic pill to fix every behavior under the sun does not exist, but some pills can help you get a leg up on significant behavior problems.

"Max Von Sydow" needs behavior modification medication as part of his daily routine. He loves his owner, Dan Maher of Dan Maher Stained Glass in Cambridge Massachusetts, where Max can be seen working by Dan's side- when he's not taking a personal day at the beach. Photo credit: Becky Cyr.

Here are some examples where behavior modification medication can help a dog that is also working with a plan written by a vet behaviorist, a certified professional trainer, applied animal behaviorist, or certified behavior consultant:

Separation Anxiety: If your dog barks when you leave, you might have a training issue. Your dog might be bored or has taken it upon himself to play "bark at the neighbors" while you're absent. However, if your dog breaks his teeth on the crate to come find you, is bleeding, stress pants, digs in the crate, defecates, or is otherwise having a significant emotional response to being left alone, behavior modification medication might be recommended with a training plan.

Thunderstorm Phobia: If your dog shakes, pants, is hyper-vigilant, and has an elevated heart rate during a thunderstorm, call a positive reinforcement dog trainer. Keep in mind that aversive training with phobias exacerbates the problem. The trainer will likely recommend a desensitization program and might recommend medication to help the training stick, if the anxiety is significant, or if there are other anxieties present in addition to thunderstorm phobia.

Noise Phobias: In addition to thunderstorm phobia (where the sound of the thunder, plus the little shocks that they get from static electricity can cause a significant fear response), some dogs are fearful of vacuum cleaners, garbage trucks, doors opening and closing in an apartment building, loud footsteps, buses stopping, garbage bins falling over...the list is endless. If your dog is more sensitive to noises than you feel is normal, call a certified dog trainer to assess what's going on. It might be a game for your dog, it might be lack of exercise, or it might be a legitimate anxiety that can be helped with medication and a training plan.

Global Anxiety Disorder: I am seeing more and more of these dogs in the city. There is no singular reason why this is occurring, but I suspect it's a complex combination: mis-matching issue to family and environment; genetics and health of the dog in question, regardless of location; dogs not socialized to the city living in urban centers; and dogs not having enough outlets are just a few possible reasons. That, and five years ago I wasn't seeing behavior cases, whereas now I am, so my glasses might be colored a little differently for that reason alone.

Regardless if it's my perception, or an actual *thing,* this is still one of the most challenging anxieties imaginable. These dogs are afraid to be left alone, they can't cope with any new stimulus, they are hyper-vigilant all the time, and they are balls of tense muscle and fur. They can't cope with anything new. I am convinced that their inner dialog is "Outside, outside is scary, but the walls inside are scary, too. I hear something! Did you hear that? Oh, it was my food dish. Whew, ok....wait, did you hear that? That was a car, two blocks away. What if they are coming to get me! Don't leave me alone, I can't do this alone. Oh, great, cats—oh my god, the cats—they have daggers IN THEIR FEET!"

Dogs suffering from Global Anxiety Disorder, or similar disorders, tend to benefit from behavior modification medication regardless of whether they are in the city or the country. Talk to your vet.

Compulsive Disorders: Technically, we can't call this behavior "OCD" or *obsessive compulsive disorder* because *obsessive* is considered a human term. Humans can obsess, and there is some evidence out there that suggests dogs might obsess, too (in our house, we call it OCDD: obsessive compulsive disc disorder). Until more studies come out, the medical term for dogs is *compulsive disorder*, because we can only observe the compulsive act.

Compulsive disorder is a medical condition that needs to be diagnosed by a veterinarian or certified behavior specialist. Behaviors can include compulsive licking, spinning, light or shadow chasing, air snapping (it might look like the dog is catching invisible flies), and other repetitive acts in which the dog cannot be distracted. In severe cases, the dog can cause significant physical harm to himself, but still can't stop the behavior. Many of these dogs need to be placed on behavior modification medication and follow a strict behavior plan for the rest of their lives.

These compulsive disorders are often linked to certain dog breeds, though not all dogs in that breed have compulsive disorder, and not all compulsive disorders are specific to a dog breed. For example: Dobermans are often diagnosed with compulsive licking, in some cases to the point of bleeding, but that doesn't mean that all Dobermans will have compulsive disorder. Nor does it mean that a Maltese can't suffer from the same disorder. See a certified behavior specialist for assistance with this very serious issue.

If you have an interest in holistic approaches, talk with your veterinarian and see if she has recommendations, or talk with a behavior specialist who has an interest in holistic approaches. While these remedies might or might not work for your particular animal, in most cases they won't hurt. There may be a shorter recovery time when holistics are used *in tandem* with traditional medications and a behavior plan in place. I can attest that massage therapy did help Sadie in partnership with the medication, a behavior plan and routine training outside of the home. Even as a dog trainer, I still needed to take her to off-site training as part of her treatment. I know several dogs that have improved with acupuncture and herbal treatments with a behavior plan in place.

I also have had a handful of students who thought they were dealing with behavior issues, only to find out that their dog had Lyme disease or other physical issues that were fixed with medication and a health plan. No matter how hard we train, we can't train out Lyme, which is why you need to see your vet first.

Medication can be a tough call for dog owners. Trainers and behaviorists are often met with resistance when medication is recommended, but if your dog is really suffering this can be a way to help your dog find peace. That is something that all dog owners want for their pets. When a dog suffers from coughing or limping, we give them a pill. When they are having a very real response to stimuli or have a disorder that can be aided by the use of behavior modification medication with a training plan, the difference in that dog and that family can be night and day. It's not for every dog or every situation, but for the circumstances where it is used, medication can be a lifesaver (quite literally) for the dog.

Harnesses, Head Collars and Choke Chains, Oh My!

How to pick the right walking gear for a city dog

There are almost as many tools to walk your dog as there are breeds of dogs! There are front-clip harnesses, pulling harnesses, collars, martingale collars, choke chains, prong collars, head collars and that's just to name a few. Not all of these contraptions will help you walk your dog. For starters, most harnesses that buckle at the back actually encourage pulling behavior, which is the opposite behavior most people want. How do you know what tool is the best for your particular dog? Here is a list of the broader categories of equipment you might come across as it relates to walking your dog, and how to pick the best device for your particular situation.

- Buckle Collar
- Martingale/Sight hound Collars
- Harnesses: Front and Back
- Head Collar
- Choke Chains
- Prong Collars

Buckle Collar:

Whether or not you decide to use a different aid to walk your dog, I can't stress enough the importance of a collar for hosting dog tags. Imagine your black lab dashes out of the front door or runs away at the park. It's a lot harder to tell the public to look out for a black lab without a collar, than a black lab with a red collar, blue bandana, and green tags. If your dog is picked up by animal control or a Good Samaritan, identification tags are going to be an important step in having Fido returned to you. In short, whether you walk your dog with a collar, or you use another device, always keep a collar on your dog with identification, city license, and a rabies tag. If the I.D. tag falls off, the dog can still be tracked using the rabies tag number and the city license number, so make sure to keep all of these on your dog. These are all visual markers that make it significantly easier to identify a dog, especially if he's a common breed.

If the sound of jangling tags annoys you, or if your dog sets off other dogs in the neighborhood with his ringing dog tags, there is a product called Quiet Spot®. Simply place the tags on the dog's collar as you typically would. Then, put the Quiet Spot® pouch over the tags, encasing them in a soft pouch that is secured by Velcro. There are other products out there that are inexpensive and effective for silencing dog tags, but I can speak personally to the effectiveness of this magic little pouch.

"But My Dog Has A Microchip. He Doesn't Need ID Tags"

A microchip is a tool commonly used to identify lost animals. It's about the size of a grain of rice and is placed under the skin of the dog or cat between the shoulder blades. It's highly recommended by vets, rescue groups, shelters, trainers, and behavior experts. Getting a microchip can take place during any procedure when the pet is under anesthesia (including spay or neuter), or in the office during a routine visit without anesthesia.

The microchip does *not* replace a standard collar with identification tags. I've had students over the years elect not to have a collar and tags, despite the dog slipping out of the harness or running away. If the dog is lost and he is scanned at a vet's office or shelter, then the microchip has done its duty. That said, the microchip is a backup method of finding your dog. It is not a GPS system to ping your dog and it will not be a visually useful method of identifying your pet, unlike a bright collar that can be used to help identify your dog at a distance. Find a pretty collar (or a manly collar!) and keep ID tags for your dog on the collar. Always. Even with the use of other walking apparatuses.

Martingale Collar/Greyhound Collar/Modified Slip Collar:

These are names for the same kind of collar. I love these collars. They are so pretty.

Zeppelin wearing a Martingale Collar from Beez Louise Designs, and the Quiet Spot® tag silencer.

Dogs that have a skinny head and particularly wide neck, like the greyhound above, can back out of a standard collar even if it's fitted correctly. The cure for "Houdini" is to tighten a standard collar to the point

of constant tension (which is not recommended), or to purchase one of these little numbers. When fitted properly, these collars are very loose in the absence of tension around the neck, but if the dog backs up or springs forward suddenly, they tighten to a set point to prevent escaping. These are not designed to be used as a "training collar" or as an aversive device. These are strictly to prevent a dog from escaping. Unlike a slip lead or choke chain, these collars have a built in stop mechanism so they won't choke the dog if fitted appropriately. If you have questions about sizing, consult a trainer, or read this:
http://www.collargirl.com/how_martingale_work.htm

Harnesses:

In every single class I teach, I have at least one person show up with her dog straining to get into my classroom. It doesn't matter if the dog is 20 pounds or 80 pounds—the result is always the same. The owner is invariably trailing behind and in a panicky voice utters, "I hope we cover loose leash walking!" Without fail, this dog is wearing a harness that clips to the back.

There are thousands of harnesses to choose from. Some claim they are no-pull, some are nylon and stretchy, and many are just too darned cute. Some are step-in harnesses, and some slide over the head of the dog. The possibilities are endless! So which ones stop pulling?

"Just pullin'. Don't care!"
Kaiju wears his stretchy harness. Luckily for Nobuko Ichikawa, he walks really well on this device and isn't a strong puller, unlike his husky relatives!

We've all seen the really comfortable, nylon and mesh harness on dogs where the leash clips to the back. Some of these harnesses are stretchy and are padded in all the right places. Compare those harnesses to the ones that competitive sled dogs and competitive pulling dogs wear: These harnesses also clip to the back of the dog, are stretchy and are padded in all the right places. Using a similar harness design that competitive dog sledders use is not the best way to discourage your dog from pulling on walks. Back-clip harnesses tend to encourage pulling, which will make your job a lot harder.

If you have a dog that walks beautifully on leash, that doesn't pull and is trained to walk with you, a standard back attach harness might be a good option. Our greyhound walked with a back clip harness because he never pulled on leash and he had a neck injury that was aggravated when he walked with the leash attached to his collar. Conversely, if walking your dog feels like a form of medieval torture, you might wish to try a harness designed to take some of the ease out of the pull (and your rotator cuff).

SENSE-ation® Front-Clip Harness as modeled by Moose.
The leash clips to the front, making it harder for this peppy pug to pull.

Front-Clip Harnesses.

Front-clip harnesses are exactly what the name indicates. The leash attaches to the chest of the dog instead of to the back. When a dog pulls, his forward momentum is temporarily stopped. These harnesses are very adjustable, and several brands fit over the dog's head, which is significantly easier than trying to pull a dog's legs through the bottom of the harness. For most handlers, this is the selling point! Examples of these simple designs include the SENSE-ation® Harness (photo above) and the Easy Walk® Harness (photo below).

It's important to note that with any chest attach harness, if you don't teach your dog what you want instead of pulling, your dog might learn to pull even with the "no pull" features. Check out the Victoria Stilwell four part series on loose leash walking, which is available for free on YouTube, so you can start a training regimen with the new device.

Some harnesses work better than others for particular body types. For example, the Easy Walk® doesn't work as well on skinny dogs or puppies, but tends to work better on dogs with a broader chest, like a Rottweiler. If the front piece sags or loosens up on walks, clip the leash through both the harness loop and the dogs collar, or try another front-clip harness, like the SENSE-ation®, Freedom Harness® or Comfortflex Harness®.

*Bela and her owner, Cindy Robinson move with ease
with the help of an Easy-Walk Harness®*

Chafing is sometimes an issue with shorter haired dogs with any harness, but there are front-clip harnesses that are able to accommodate the no-pull feature while also offering padding under the front legs to prevent rubbing (the Halti™/Holt™ Brand harness prevents chafing, as does the Freedom Harness®). As I recommend to my students, start with the Easy Walk® or the SENSE-ation®, find the features you like, and then do an online search for additional features once you know what you are looking for.

Sporn® No-Pull Mesh Harness:
Of course, there is one in every group that goes against the grain. Though this is a back clip harness, it's designed to lift the front legs up when the dog pulls. Some dogs are sensitive to the pressure put on the back, which stops the dog from wanting to pull, but other dogs really don't mind that pressure at all. The downside is that this can chafe, as many of these harnesses can on shorter haired breeds, and if your dog doesn't seem to mind his legs leaving the ground when pulling then this harness isn't the right one for you. However, the leash is less likely to get caught under the front legs when using this harness, particularly on shorter dogs, which is a downside of all the front-clip harnesses listed above.

Pros to Using No-Pull Harnesses:
- The leash attaches to a ring on the chest (or, in very few cases, the back, though most back-clip harnesses encourage pulling) leaving the esophagus, airway and neck vertebrae at minimal risk of injury.
- Some dogs miraculously walk with no further training when walking on a harness designed to assist in ceasing pulling behaviors, though I recommend continuing teaching all dogs how to walk properly, even with a device on.
- For dogs with spinal injuries or other medical conditions, this is a good alternative to walking on a standard issue collar.
- Many of the front-clip harnesses slide comfortably over the head of the dog, which means no more pulling the harness over the front legs.

Cons to No-Pull Harnesses:
- If you have the wrong harness or an ill-fitting harness, it can encourage pulling behaviors, making it difficult to walk your dog.
- Step-In Harnesses are inconvenient to get on and off a dog.
- Some of these harnesses can cause chafing in some shorter haired dogs, though some designs, like the Freedom Harness® and the Halti™ Harness, are changing the designs to prevent chafing.
- The leash is likely to get caught under the front legs with front-clip harnesses if you aren't mindful of the leash, or have a short-statured dog.
- Some experts note that ill-fitting chest clip harnesses can create structural damage, so make sure that you have the right harness for your dog. Regardless, if the dog is walking with a loose leash, then this injury risk is nullified.

Head Collars:
It's no secret that I'm a big fan of head collars. Not all trainers are, but these are a tool I really advocate for. They're not for every handler and they're not for every dog, but nothing is right for every handler or every dog.

I grew up in Maine where everyone joined 4-H and handled livestock. I also rode horses as soon as I could walk. Livestock and farm animals are moved most easily by the use of a head collar, or halter. It's much easier to convince a 1,600 pound horse to move with you when you have it by the nose. Dogs are the only animals we expect to walk perfectly by a wrapping something around their necks. If you don't believe me, try taking a cat for a walk with a collar. Go on – I'll wait!

We've come a long way. Just a few years ago, most people would stop me on the street and ask if Sadie's head collar was a muzzle. While some designs do have that function built in, the head collar is predominantly a piece of equipment designed to help you walk your excited, frustrated, giant, or pulling-breed dog without tearing your rotator cuff or causing irreparable damage to a dog's trachea. Most people now understand that it's a tool to walk an excited dog safely.

A note of caution regarding any head collar: Do not use these headpieces with anything other than a four or six foot leash. Do not use a head collar if you are doing long line recalls or if you walk your dog on a retractable leash. If your dog takes off at speed and comes to a sudden stop, their head can twist which can cause sprains to the neck, or worse. If you are prone to "leash popping" your dog, a head collar might not be appropriate for you. As with any device, it might not be appropriate for all dogs, or all handlers.

If fitted properly and in the hands of a skilled pro, you can get great, near-immediate results. However, if you just toss the head collar on a fearful dog and expect it to go without a hitch, you might be in for a bad experience, and some dogs, no matter what, will flail like a fish. Jean Donaldson has a wonderful YouTube video on how to get most dogs to love the head piece (http://www.youtube.com/watch?v=1wakterNyUg). She moves slowly and goes over everything you need to be successful when fitting and using the device. This is my preferred method of walking strong pullers, reactive or aggressive dogs, and exuberant jumpers. It's a fantastic alternative to other devices.

Bella is wearing her Gentle Leader® with a homemade safety strap.
She is owned by Alexandra Vitug of Vellejo California

Gentle Leader®
    The Gentle Leader® is a head piece made by Premier®. This is the head collar most people know by name. As Kleenex® is to tissue, Gentle Leader® is to head collars. However, this is my least favorite device of those covered, though still a great device.

Pros:
- Commercially available at most box-store pet shopping centers.
- Very adjustable.
- Variety of colors.

Cons:
- Not appropriate for short-snout dogs, such as the pug, Old English bulldog, and other dogs that are brachycephalic.
- No extra padding on the bridge of the nose, so some dogs might chafe.
- There is no safety strap. If the dog escapes from the head piece, you are left holding the leash and head collar as Fido runs away. You would have to create a safety strap modeled after the other brands, or use a second leash at all times.
- No extra side straps for stability.
- Since this is such a simple design, you have to have the head piece super-snug to prevent the dog from escaping out of the device, which can be uncomfortable.

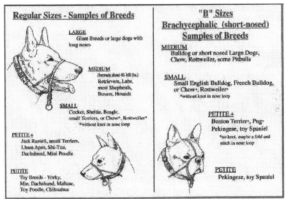

Diagram of the Snoot Loop™ via http://www.snootloop.com/

Snoot Loop™

This product is the go-to head halter for dogs that have short snouts, or dogs that don't fit the other headpieces very well. Trainers and behavior specialists have been recommending this piece for years. I really wish these were in box stores, because they are a fantastic tool.

Pros:
- This halter is by far the most adjustable. It also has an additional strap that crosses over the forehead for short snouted dogs.

- There are multiple points of adjustment, making this the least likely to chafe of all the brands mentioned here, and the hardest to escape from.
- There is a collar attached as part of the design (you can see a thicker strap on the dog above, behind his ears). This also is a safety feature, so if your dog does manage to escape from the snout loop, you still have your dog attached by leash, unlike the Gentle Leader®.
- It has a muzzle feature if the dog lunges, but only if you use tension in the leash in a very specific way. Otherwise, it will function as a walking device only.

Cons:
- Your dog looks like Hannibal Lecter.
- Though it has multiple points of adjustment, it can be hard to adjust initially. This could be a 'pro' in that it's harder for the dog to wiggle the piece out of position.
- Not commercially available—have to find it online.

Sadie wearing her Halti™ during a very wet outdoor wedding ceremony.
Photo by Emily Sterne of Emily Sterne Photography

Halti™/Holt™:
These headpieces are the best of all worlds: affordable, easy to fit, easy to adjust, and easy to put on. A word of caution: if you have a dog with a short snout or a dog that needs something a little sturdier, you might need a different head collar.

Pros:
- Commercially available at big box stores.
- Padding over the nose strap, lessening the likelihood of chafing.

140

- Built in safety strap that attaches back to the dog's collar. In the event the dog escapes from the head piece, you still have your dog connected by the collar to the leash.
- Convenient as the Gentle Leader®, but more sturdy.
- Has a minor muzzle option for dogs that lunge aggressively, but to be clear, it is not a muzzle substitute for dogs that really need a muzzle.

Cons:
- Not as adjustable as the Snoot Loop™, so it might be hard to find the perfect size for your particular dog.
- Sizing is rather generous. If you have a big dog for the breed, use the manufacturer's recommendation. However, if you have a smaller dog for breed standard, or a female, you might actually want to get the size below the recommendation on the back of the package.
- Some dogs can still chafe. The nose piece might ride up and irritate the dog's eyes.
- Not appropriate for dogs with a short snout.

Canny Collar®:
   One downside to all of the above headpieces is that they buckle underneath the dogs chin. As a result, dogs often step over the leash and get tangled if you're not holding the leash correctly, or if you have a very short dog. The Canny Collar® fixes this issue by connecting the lead to the back of the neck (like a collar!) but adding the functionality of a headpiece.

Pros:
- Connects behind the dog's head to the leash, so the leash shouldn't get wrapped under the dog's leg as you walk.
- Can't twist the dog's neck because of leash placement, though never use this device if you are doing long line recalls or use a flexi-leash.
- It's easy to put on.
- Safety strap/additional collar like the Snoot Loop™.

Cons:
- Harder to get than the Gentle Leader® or Halti™, but you can purchase online.
- Dogs can back out of the snout piece, but you still have your dog by the collar because of the safety strap, if fitted correctly.
- Not appropriate for dogs with a short snout.

Tesla shows off her Canny Collar® – one of the few head collars that attach to the back of the head instead of under the chin. Tess is owned by Jessica Fry, KPA-CTP, and her husband, Jacob Strauss of Roslindale, Massachusetts.

As with any walking equipment, talk with your trainer to see what equipment might be most appropriate for you and your dog specifically. Maybe a harness is a more appropriate tool or maybe your dog just needs to work on exercises designed to teach proper leash skills. When in doubt, ask your trainer.

Choke Chains and Prong Collars

There is a lot of controversy regarding the use of prongs and choke chains for walking and training dogs. I've seen excellent handlers use prongs or chokes, and their dogs seem totally fine. I've seen terrible handlers use prongs on their dogs and the dogs are "totally fine" in that they aren't pulling, but they display signs of being incredibly stressed out. I've seen excellent handlers use prongs and chokes on sensitive dogs, and their dogs are riddled with anxiety. I've seen terrible handlers use prongs and chokes on sensitive dogs, and the dogs are just a mess.

Much of the debate on prongs and choke chains comes from decades of using chokes as the primary training device in every class across the country. Since those dogs ended up totally fine, why change course now? Anecdotally, if you are the owner of a dog that can "handle" a choke chain and have never had a problem, then you would be unlikely to change to another device. Humans, like dogs, will do what has proven to work over time.

The downsides to chokes and prongs far outweigh the upsides. On the one hand, if you have a dog that is pulling, and you have excellent timing, are using effective punishment techniques, and are teaching the dog what you want him to do (not just yanking him back while saying "heel"), these devices can work remarkably fast. They continue to exist because they can be mighty effective for a pulling dog, if you know what you're doing. On the other hand, if you are not actively teaching your dog what you want him to do instead, and he's just getting choked or pinched every time he sees something exciting, the dog could start to associate interesting things with pain. Pain leads to fear, and fear turns to shyness or aggression.

Case in point: Sadie used to love other dogs. When we moved to the city, she would play with other dogs and she even enjoyed the local dog park. When I ended up on crutches, I had no idea about head collars or harnesses. I popped her in a prong collar to make sure she couldn't pull me over while I hobbled behind her. I really thought I was teaching her to walk. After one week on the prong, Sadie's behavior around other dogs started to deteriorate. She'd wag her tail, but growl and lunge at dogs when she got close. This was the beginning of her reactivity, and later outright aggression, to other dogs.

In the interest of full disclosure, there were several things at play here: Sadie had a history of anxiety, so this device amplified what anxiety she already had. Additionally, I wasn't teaching her what I wanted her to do. I did what most beginners with a prong tend to do, which is to keep a tight enough leash and let the collar do all the work. Had we been in the country, she *might* have been totally fine, since there wouldn't have been as many dogs for her to get excited about, and consequently, jump out in front of me and get pronged. In the city, there is a dog every two blocks. These dogs are barking dogs, running dogs, dogs walking on leash, dogs in windows and anywhere you can imagine a dog. Every single time she stepped forward to investigate, she was met with a painful squeezing around her neck. It didn't take long for such a sensitive, aware dog to make a connection: "Dogs hurt my neck. I'll hurt them before they can hurt me."

And lo, on the 7th day, we had created aggression.

Vets agree, for the most part, that there are better tools available. Choke chains have no stopping mechanism. Therefore, you can literally choke a dog until it passes out from asphyxiation. Cesar Millan famously asphyxiated a "dominant aggressive" husky, which put the animal community up in arms—and not just for making a dog pass out due to lack of oxygen. The terminology "dominant aggression" is grossly misunderstood and misused on television and in society. Dogs that are walked on choke chains often continue to pull, even through wheezing and pain. The wheezing owners report to vets and trainers is the sound of injury to a dog's trachea. That sound absolutely shouldn't be ignored, even if your dog continues to pull.

All animals have an opposition reflex. Think of a game of tug-o-war. When you feel the rope tug, you instinctively pull back. The same principle applies to dogs and all mammals. If pulling gets a dog where he wants to go, he will continue to pull, even through pain. This increases the likelihood of neck "hardware" issues, such as: damaged trachea, larynx, spinal tissues, and soft tissue damage. Some dogs even suffer from Horner's Syndrome, a neurological condition. Droopy eyelids, sagging muscles in the eyes and face, constricted pupils, prolapsed third eyelid, and an eye that appears to be sunken in, are all symptoms of Horner's syndrome. Though this is often idiopathic (without known cause), there appear to be links between choke chains, prongs, and other events that can cause trauma to the neck and spinal cord.

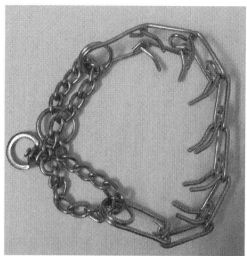

Prong Collar / German Pinch Collar
Photo by Alison Macdonald

Prongs, like choke chains, use pain to theoretically prevent a dog from engaging in a behavior. Great care should be taken when justifying the use of pain as a training technique. Science clearly illustrates that other techniques are far less harmful to the dog, and work better. An ill-timed leash correction or using the device too harshly can irreparably damage a dog mentally and physically. Any device can cause pain and irritation. Front-clip harnesses can chafe or annoy a dog that can't get to where he wants to go, but that is, at most, annoying to the dog. Contrast this minor frustration to the lifelong scars around a dog's neck when a prong collar is used inappropriately, and we're talking apples to machetes.

Of the two, prongs at least have a stopping mechanism, like a martingale collar. When sized correctly, this feature exists to prevent a dog from choking or having significant physical damage done to neck tissue. Contrast that with a choke chain or slip lead, which does not have such a stop feature. I've seen dogs literally spin around and get caught by another dog's teeth and choke; I've seen owners try to get compliance and hang their dog by accident; and in one terrible incident, I came across a husky that had been left unattended by an irresponsible groomer in the back room of a facility where I once worked. The dog was tethered to a doorknob with a slip lead (a leash and choke chain device made out of nylon). He panicked, spun in such a way that his paws got around his leash, and his weight tightened the leash around his neck. When I found

144

him, his tongue was already blue. He ended up physically ok, but he really never felt hunky dory about coming back to visit that negligent groomer—gee, I wonder why? I never went back, either.

Choke Chain
Photo by Alison Macdonald

Call me silly, but I believe we should teach our dogs what we want them to do, instead of just insisting they don't do things that irritate us. It's on us to train our dogs in the same way walking, feeding, and cleaning poop off the sidewalk is our job. It's something we do willingly when we get our new best friends, and we owe it to them, I feel, to do so without archaic devices that science expressly states stress them out and increase anxiety. Don't even get me started on electric shock collars. I tend not to learn much when I'm stressed out, and I know the same was true for my dog. I just don't understand why we think these devices are ok to put on our dogs, but we would never think to put something like them on our cats, horses, sheep, or coworkers. Dogs are the only animals we walk by the neck, and the only domestic animal we try to "teach" with shocks, chokes and prongs, yet they still curl up with us at night. Sometimes I wonder what it is that humans did to deserve the companionship of dogs, because things like this would undermine any other relationship. Man's best friend, indeed.

If you decide to continue to use these devices, make sure your dog also wears a standard collar with appropriate identification at all times. Prong and choke collars should not be used as an alternative to a regular collar. They can get caught on things, or get tangled during play, which can lead to significant pain, injury, or worse. **Never**—let me repeat—**never** leave a dog unattended while wearing these devices, and always take them off during play, after walks, and after training.

My Dog Won't Walk

Um, my dog is broken. He hates walks. What do I do?

Most people just wish their dogs would walk on a leash without pulling; however, there are some dogs that just won't walk at all. In every class of six dogs, there are usually four who will pull so hard it's painful to watch, one who walks wonderfully without any encouragement, and one who refuses to move. This is incredibly disappointing to owners who wanted a walking buddy.

Jasmine, a 13-year-old rescued basset hound, is happy sitting right here, taking in all of the sights and smells. Why walk when she is with her love, owner Kerri Silva?

Some dogs pull hard enough that they choke themselves walking, or owners get dragged down the street for every pee-break. That isn't a pleasant experience for either party and can lead to complications down the road (physical injury to the neck and spinal cord, frustration on leash, and other issues covered in the previous chapter). On the other hand, there are some dogs that just want to stop and smell the roses, and the sidewalk, and the trees, and the grass, and the list goes on. What do you do when your dog just doesn't want to walk?

My Dog Is Terrified To Go Outside /
My Dog Doesn't Like New Walking Routes:

If your dog falls under the category of "doesn't like to walk," it's important to figure out why your dog isn't walking. Is it too hot or cold for your particular dog? Is your dog really scared or nervous around buses, kids, traffic, and trash cans knocked over by the wind? Alternatively, is your dog just a slow mover and is the poster child for "stop and smell the roses"?

For dogs that are anxious or nervous about going outside, I recommend hiring a certified professional to come into the home. This is to assess what's happening in your environment, and condition your dog to acclimate to the environment. It can be a lot for a new dog that isn't used to the city to suddenly find himself in a metropolis, or even suburbia. As much as I would love to say that dogs just get over fear, they typically don't. Things tend to get worse without help and a tangible plan.

I want you to sit in silence, turn off the television and just close your eyes. Listen to all of the things happening right this minute. For instance, I hear a rumbling truck outside of my window. I hear the busy traffic of a typical morning commute on the highway. I hear my clock ticking. I hear a dog barking two houses down, and sirens wailing across the street. I hear Sadie snoring, my landlord downstairs doing laundry, his girlfriend walking with high heels upstairs and an airplane overhead.

This is a lot for a dog to take in, a dog that has superior hearing to humans, superior smell (I don't even want to know what Somerville smells like to a dog), and that sees movement much more vividly than we do. It's no wonder our dogs, when left to their own devices, take up hobbies like barking, guarding, and in some cases, hiding in the bathroom. If these are the issues you are experiencing, and your dog is nervous walking down the street (tail tucked, shaking, sitting alert and refusing to move), then call for help. This won't get better on its own, and it won't get better if you force your dog to walk with you. You can worsen the issue greatly, and make life harder on both you and your dog. Be patient and call a certified professional for assistance and guidance.

My Dog Isn't Anxious. He's Just a Slow Mover and Sniffs Everything:

The first question that I ask students regarding dogs that just like to sniff everything is, "Who is this walk *for?*" Consider that many dogs are in the home for most of the day and are unable to really entertain themselves. When they are finally afforded time outside, some just want to run around and check out everything, but others are perfectly content to partake in the doggie equivalent of reading the morning paper. "Yippee—smells, sights, and sounds to take in!"

The first thing many people do every morning is check their email. Our dogs don't have that luxury. They have to wait for us to let them outside to explore and to engage all of their senses. Going outside to sniff is a great experience for them. It's healthy. Dogs get an amazing amount of information from every flower, tree, and fire hydrant they sniff. They can smell the dog that walked by two minutes ago, as well as the dog that walked by two weeks ago. Their nose is as critical to them as our eyes are to us. A sniffy walk for many dogs is like taking in Tolstoy: it's mentally engaging, relaxing and satisfying to them, and they need it.

Yes, walking is important exercise for both dogs and people, and it's a fantastic bonding experience, but consider the bonding experience from the dogs' perspective. If walking is a moderately paced two miles because *you* can walk a set route in 30 minutes listening to music, but your dog is being dragged the entire way, it's not really a bonding experience for either participant. The handler is stressed, because "We need exercise, and walking is exercise." The dog is stressed because "Hey, smell these...wait! Ok, let me pull up to this tree and...ouch! I was sniffing that!" Neither dog, nor owner, is enjoying the walk.

The plan for this overly sniffy behavior should never include dragging the dog behind you until he complies. Additionally, yelling at the dog out of frustration will probably backfire. Dogs tend to sniff *more* when they are stressed out as a calming signal to you, so if you are frustrated, your dog is more likely to slow down, sniff more, and tune you out—all behaviors that are contributing to you getting more frustrated. This is a classic feedback loop, and the best way to stop a feedback loop is to come up with another solution.

Letting canines run energy off, sprint, zip, play, and bomb around with other dogs, if they can handle that activity, is just as important to their overall mental health as sniffing is on walks. If you have a really sniffy dog that won't walk at all because it's so fixated on sniffing, and it takes over 30 minutes to get around a city block, there are people who can come and help with that.

In cases like this, I tend to recommend finding a hobby for the dog and owner, like tracking, or Nosework™ games. Search and Rescue (http://www.sardogsus.org/) and NASAR (http://nasar.org) are two sites for the mighty ambitious. If you can give your dog an outlet where he is able to sniff to his heart's content, with a directive, the dog will likely be more focused overall. Additionally, you learn how to use sniffing as a reward for good walking behavior, which means that walks can change dramatically for the better for both parties.

Perhaps structuring walks to allow periods of sniffing and periods of walking is the answer for an overly sniffy hound. Alternatively, a head collar can help keep your dog focused on walking with you, or use a long line on a harness instead of a six-foot leash to give your pup a little extra sniff time while you keep trucking along (though never use anything other than a six-foot leash if you are using a head collar). Perhaps running to your dog's favorite spot to sniff is enough exercise, aerobically and mentally, for both you and your pup. There are plenty of plans that can be catered to you and your dog.

Also, consider just letting your dog sniff, and change what a walk means for you. Walking is a great activity for dogs, but many dogs get more mental stimulation out of sniffing on walks than physical exercise anyway. If you have a particularly excited dog, a walk isn't going to burn off the energy aerobically, so a run might be more appropriate for exercise. Still, it's important to take a couple of short sniffy walks with dogs every day, and let them check their pee-mail.

If you really want to go for a walk for your own health, and your dog is too arthritic, or sniffy for your own personal desires, sync up your iPod and go for a longer walk sans Fido. Save 20-30 minutes to bond with your dog a couple times a day and let your dog sniff on these special outings. If pulling is a problem, read the previous chapter on equipment to help you, seek a positive reinforcement trainer to visit your home, take a class on loose leash walking from an accredited trainer, or watch the four part Victoria Stilwell series on loose leash walking, which is available for free on YouTube.

Try "sniffy walks" for a week, and see how your dog's attitude changes. You might be pleasantly surprised to find out that the solution to frenetic energy was to let your dog sniff all along.

A Note on Back Yards

There is more to life than a back yard!

We had neighbors in East Somerville who had the nicest dog. We'd walk by their house with our dogs, and the young pup would play bow (a form of dog body language indicating playfulness) and try to engage us from behind her fence. Most of the time, we'd say hi, but we wouldn't hang out for long. We didn't know these neighbors, and we didn't want to bother their dog. Over the next few months, the pup's greetings went from playful to whining—"oh PLEEEEASE play with me! I'm here all alone! PLEEEEEEEEEEEEEEASE!"

We suffered that frigid winter in our home and didn't go on our typical longer walks, as most people in New England can sympathize with. When spring broke, we went on our first walk beyond our block and passed the fence with the young pup that had become an adolescent dog. She charged the fence aggressively and barked with frustration and anger. There was no owner in sight. She was just left outside to entertain herself, often all day long. When people and dogs walked by, her excitement turned to frustration, which turned to reactivity and barrier aggression. We got to see the transition in person because this was a dog in our neighborhood, but a dog like this exists in most neighborhoods.

This happens in many households, particularly those with fenced-in back yards (in the country, dogs that are chained to a dog house all day can exhibit the same behaviors). It's tempting to leave the dogs alone, or use the fenced yard as a replacement for walks.

Back yards can be a great tool, especially if they are fenced in. You can play find it games with food, toss a ball, let your dog out for a quick pee break, and some rescue groups will not let you adopt a pet without a fenced in back yard. However, dogs just left to their own devices outside without supervision can get into a lot of trouble. If you live in a city, you've likely been barked at by a dog in a window or behind a fence. Barrier aggression (the barking, growling, pacing, and "watchdog" behavior of a dog that is held back by a barrier) is already a huge issue in the city, and it's not worth the risk of eviction caused by a barking dog, or irritating your neighbors. Do yourself a favor and don't leave Fido outside to fend for herself. Stay outside with your dog and make sure your dog isn't causing trouble, or better yet, play with your dog and prevent this behavior from even starting. Every time the dog is outside you should be, too, and you should be doing something together.

*Lilah howls, "helloooooooo!" to her owner, Pat Dains
of On The Run – a dog playgroup service in Somerville, MA.*

In addition to barking concerns, there's also the risk of a dog becoming an escape artist. Some dogs will dig under fences, jump over them, or will find a way to climb out.

We had the experience of two giant Labradors jump their fence to greet us across the street, which was a problem because the Labradors were in the middle of an urban street, and my dogs needed space from even the friendliest, goofiest retrievers. We were all lucky that the owner was outside with these dogs and was able to come and get them, though she was calling for them to "come" with zero success. Even Sadie's vocal protests to her space being invaded were not a deterrent for these two *happy* dogs. It's important to note that I was irritated that my dogs' space was not respected and that her dogs could have been hit by a car. She was irritated that her dogs wouldn't come back when she called them and that they could have been hit by a car.

We were both concerned for her dogs in the street and for my dogs that were trapped. What we both walked away with was a feeling of "that guy." I thought "Why doesn't she just raise her fence? Can't she just teach her dogs to come? Couldn't she see her dogs were in danger, not just from oncoming traffic, but from my dog that was trying to bite hers? Sadie needs space or she'll bite. It'll be her fault if her dogs get bitten."

She was thinking "Why does she walk that aggressive dog? Where does she get off telling me that I have to raise my fence or call my dogs? Can't she see my dogs are friendly? They weren't hit by a car, so they are fine. They just wanted to say hi. She's lucky her dog didn't bite mine, or she'd be in trouble."

Maybe you can relate to one (or both!) sides of this situation. We all deal with issues like this in the city. It's easy to just walk away without resolving anything. The long and the short of it is that we are all entitled to our space with our dogs. We just have to share this space and respect everyone's right to that shared space. I'd argue that we both had a right to our opinion of what happened but this really could have been prevented with a little understanding on both sides of the argument – after all, we both were concerned for all the dogs in the situation. Luckily no one was hurt or hit by a car, which really would have changed everything.

All you have to do is search YouTube for "dog escapes" to get an idea of the lengths some dogs will go to taste freedom. There are impressive dogs that can scale walls and dozens of compilations of escape artists. These freedom-seeking mutts might end up picked up by Animal Control, hit by cars, or find themselves picked up by complete strangers several towns away.

The last thing to consider is that there are dozens of cases a year in Massachusetts where young dogs are picked up out of back yards when not supervised. The week that I wrote this chapter, two Rottweiler puppies were stolen out of Northern Massachusetts. One was found in an abandoned hotel room, the other is (as of this writing) still missing. I don't want to go into all the terrible things that usually happen to these dogs. You are much better off staying with your dog, making sure that she is entertained, not a nuisance to neighbors and a temptation for desperate thieves trying to make a buck off your precious pet.

How to keep your back yard "doggie proofed":
If your dog is spending time in a back yard, make sure that the following safety precautions are taken:

- Avoid pesticides and other toxic substances. Most people know that pesticides are toxic to dogs, but certain mulches can be toxic to dogs, too. Cocoa mulch is used as organic mulch with a more pleasant scent to humans but the same chemicals in dark chocolate are found in some brands of cocoa mulch. Caffeine and theobromine are the chemicals that are responsible for toxicity. Though it's possible for a dog to get sick, most dogs leave the mulch alone. However, I'd personally lean on the safe-side and not use cocoa mulch in areas where dogs have access. I've worked with dogs that have eaten rocks, chocolate, goose poop, their own poop, and other dogs' poop.

I wouldn't ever bet against the temptation of a dog eating something he shouldn't.

- Know the plants in your back yard. Fauna, such as Morning Glories, Tulips and many species in the Ivy family are toxic to dogs. There is a complete list of toxic plants to dogs—as well as parrots, horses and cats if you are into that sort of thing—at http://www.aspca.org/pet-care/animal-poison-control.
- Get a self-latching gate to make sure your pet can't get out. If you have a "Houndini," get a padlock, which prevents your dog from figuring out the latch, and prevents any humans from inadvertently opening the gate and letting your dog out.
- Make sure your pet is always attended in the back yard, so you can distract your dog when he is looking for a way out. Better yet, when you're in the back yard play with your dog.
- Check that your fence is high enough to keep your particular pet contained, especially if you have a dog that can jump over fences.
- If your dog can climb the fence, use plywood or other smooth surfaces to eliminate toe-holds.
- If your dog is prone to digging, make sure that the fence is at least 24" under the ground. You can also use chicken wire underground or place chain link fencing on the ground to prevent effective digging.
- Make sure your pet is spayed or neutered to prevent roaming behaviors associated with searching for a mate. Those dogs can be pretty determined to get out!

I would argue if your dog is able to get out of a fenced-in area with even the most basic precautions, then the dog isn't managed well enough, isn't getting enough exercise and mental stimulation or might be anxious. If your dog is particularly driven to dig under the fence, and nothing you do can prevent the behavior, call a certified professional. The same goes for compulsive jumping or climbing the fence in order to escape. There might be more to the behavior than meets the eye.

Electric Fences:
I have an interesting relationship with electric fences. I have several students who want them for their suburban back yards, which I don't ever advocate, although, I can see why students want these devices. Let me present some scenarios, all of which have happened to students or friends.

When students want an electric fence, they want it for overall good reasons. They want to give their dog more freedom to see birds, get exercise, and enjoy the sunshine. What tends to be forgotten in all of this is what it does to the dog. The temptation is there to leave the dog alone, just like with a physical fence, but there are a few additional things to consider regarding these tools.

I visited two different homes with similar presentation in the last few years. In both cases, I was called in to help with dogs that were peeing in the house and refusing to go outside. These were adult dogs that, prior to this, had no reported anxiety or history of using the "indoor facilities." In both cases it turns out that after being trained on the electric fence, the dogs regressed in their house training and refused to go outside. The shocks, "minor" as they were, happened to be just enough for both dogs to shut down and become terrified of their own back yards. It's incredibly hard to condition dogs to enjoy a space in which they were shocked for reasons they didn't understand.

I had a teacher in college tell us stories of her pup that thought squirrels outside of the electric fence were worth the consequence of the shock, but the same dog wouldn't come back into the yard because she'd get shocked. One day, the teacher ran after the dog once she left the premises. She caught the dog and had the wisdom to take the electronic collar off her dog before re-entering the yard. She did not, however, have the wisdom to turn the device off. Holding the electronic collar in one hand and her dog in the other, she zapped both of them walking back through the invisible fencing. "I never used it again after that day. It hurt and it wasn't working."

Lastly, I had a student tell me about her Siberian huskies who would sit next to the fence for hours. She couldn't figure out what they were looking at. After several hours of what appeared to be incredible patience and self-control the dogs suddenly bolted out of the electric fence. When they eventually came back home, they ran through the fence again. These dogs had figured out that the caution "beeeeeeeeeeeep" would wear out the battery, and if they waited long enough for the beeping to stop, they wouldn't get shocked. After living with huskies my entire childhood, I can absolutely see this behavior happening.

Aside from the electric shock issue, I always mention that if a predator can get in, or if your dog feels threatened, it's really hard for them to get away. In Maine, for example, if a bear can get in, and your dog can't get out, that's a problem. Skunks and porcupines can also get in. At least a physical fence can help keep predators and unwanted visitors out.

Barrier frustration is also a problem with electric fences. Just as with prong collars and choke chains, electric collars for fences or for training can unintentionally teach a dog to associate painful shocks with whatever object, person, or event is piquing their curiosity. Some dogs start to wilt and lose confidence. Some dogs aggress and become incredibly frustrated at whatever it is that is perceived to have caused an electric shock. We humans understand that certain things cause a shock to happen, but dogs don't get that. As far as they are concerned, they are just magically being electrocuted, and that feeling is painful, frustrating, and scary. It's impossible to tell which dogs are going to be ok with this training and which dogs are not.

In suburbia and in the city, there are too many distractions, too many people, too many cars, too many interesting things to keep a dog behind an invisible fence. Spend the money if you must and get a real fence, or use a long line to train your dog in more populated environments.

Socialization and Body Language

Defining socialization, how to socialize correctly, and how reading body language can prevent serious incidents

Dog owners generally know they need to socialize their new dog. The overarching idea is that the more places a puppy goes, and the more experiences a puppy has, the better off he'll be at coping in new environments later on. However, there are some things about socialization that are crucial to know, and ways to do this successfully without having it backfire down the road.

What is Socialization?

When trainers talk about socialization, they're referring to one of two different concepts. The first is the window of socialization: the critical period between birth and 16-20 weeks in which a puppy is emotionally more pliable regarding new stimuli. These ages do vary depending on the professional that you are asking and by dog breed. The general idea is that the more stuff Fido is exposed to during the socialization period, the better the dog is able to adjust to new things when it's older. For instance, if a new puppy has been socialized to passing cars, small trucks and buses, then a big truck should fit into the schema of "things that drive on the street that I can cope with."

Secondly, socialization is a verb, meaning *to socialize*. How one goes about socializing the new puppy is just as important as the window of opportunity. For starters, taking an eight-week-old puppy to the local dog park to "socialize him" can do much more harm than good if not done appropriately. Flooding (the act of essentially tossing a kid into the deep end of the pool to teach him to swim) is not the recommended method of socializing any animal, humans included. For starters, the dogs at the park should be vaccinated, but they might not be. A lot of people bring dogs that aren't suited for the dog park and if those dogs are etiquette-challenged, there is a very good chance that those are the lessons your new puppy will learn.

A more appropriate method to socialize your puppy to new dogs is to attend a socialization class or indoor playgroup where puppies are age appropriate, the floors are cleaned before and after to prevent the spread of disease, and a qualified trainer can help you decode dog body language. Is your puppy hiding and fearful? Is he jumping into the fray? Is he charging in when everyone's back is turned, but as soon as another puppy looks at him he bolts? Puppies need to build confidence, but they also should learn how to play appropriately. In the city, where there are so many dogs, so many personality types, and so many ways of determining what is safe or not safe for a dog, it's best to learn from a certified professional how to read your puppy in play and how he copes with new stimuli. Experienced professionals can teach you how to distract an over-excited puppy and also how to build confidence in a shy-guy, safely.

Your Dog Might Be Under-socialized:

The most important thing to consider is that your dog is different from all other dogs in the park, in your building, and in your past. Remember that your dog is an individual and what he or she can handle depends on each dog *individually*. Just because your previous dog loved the park, or your neighbor's dog could go up to strangers with ease, doesn't mean that this particular dog is able to go to the park or handle new experiences easily.

If your dog is afraid of men, baseball hats, or plastic bags, it doesn't necessarily indicate that your dog was abused by a man wearing a baseball hat, while carrying a plastic bag. Often, signs of under-socialization or inappropriate socialization (flooding) are similar to those found in a dog that was abused. Turning away, shaking, stiff body and other signs are all indicators that a dog either had no experience with something, which is scary, or has had a horrible experience, which is also scary. Don't assume that because your dog is scared of something that she was abused. Look at each new experience as a chance to learn something new. If your puppy is turning away, he might not have been abused, but he certainly isn't appreciating the experience, so take it down a notch. Instead of going to a busy dog park, try getting your puppy together with one buddy for a playdate to test the waters.

Every dog has a limit of what she can take. Some dogs do really well if they don't ever have to cope with things that are scary. For Sadie, coping with dogs eight feet away in an appropriate manner was as much as she could handle. As much as I wanted to push her, I would not force her to say "hi" to any dog in the interest of her comfort, my sanity, and the safety of all other dogs. Socialization does not mean that a dog will be able to handle every single experience or novelty with ease. Instead, it's more about figuring out where your dog is comfortable, where she is not comfortable, and teaching skills to cope somewhere in the middle. It's important to be able to read your dog and give her a method of coping, and also to understand that forcing her into situations in which she is stressed out, acting out, or shut-down does absolutely nothing to help her learn. Socialization is a two way street, and needs to be done *below* a threshold of physical stress for optimal learning. That point is different for every dog, and that is the missing piece when socialization goes awry.

If you have an exuberant dog that's classified as the frat boy ("Hey everyone! The party has arrived!") he can unintentionally instigate some bad behaviors in other dogs. If your dog is overwhelming other dogs, isn't playing well with others, is bullying out of excitement, or is otherwise giving off too much energy, it's best to start working with someone who can help you redirect or teach appropriate play behaviors. Alternatively, you could allow exuberant dogs to play with selected boisterous buddies instead of releasing hyper dogs into a park to practice bad manners. Socialization isn't just about learning confidence and gaining exposure to new experiences; it's also about learning manners, and it's on us as handlers to help our dogs learn.

Growling Is Good—No, Really, It Is! Trust Me!

The most important thing that every dog trainer worth their salt would tell you is to never, never, never punish a growling dog. If you punish a dog for growling, there are several things that have been missed. A growl doesn't typically come out of nowhere. A dog will stiffen, stare out of the side of his eyes, freeze, and will give very clear language that he doesn't like what's happening. When a dog growls, he is one step closer to a bite and it is also a clear signal—often the first one we listen to after ignoring all of the other clues that the dog has been giving off prior to the vocalization. If you were to punish a dog for growling, you are lessening the likelihood that the dog will growl again. However, you are also increasing the likelihood that the dog will go straight to biting, since the vocalizations have gone previously unheeded. A growl is the last line of defense: "Come no closer!" or "I don't like this! Please, listen to me!"

A dog that doesn't growl when upset is far more dangerous than one who growls when something is wrong. Growling is a warning signal, and if it is ignored, you'll lose that warning. Growling means it's time to assess what's happening, why it's happening, and to get help. Growling is not a time to hold your dog down, alpha roll him, force his mouth open to get an object, or to tell people, "He's growling but he's ok." He's not ok. Something is wrong.

If you try to take a bone from your dog, and your dog growls, think of this: what do you do when your dog tries to take food out of your hands? You would likely vocalize and in a low tone "growl" the word *no!* You might even pull the food in closer to you, stiffen your body, and intensely stare at your dog. Now think of your dog with his bone. What does he do? Does he stiffen, growl, and stare at you while pulling the desired chew closer to his body? My feeling on this is if your dog is eating or sleeping, it's best to remember the wisest words ever spoken by grandmothers everywhere: "Let sleeping dogs lie."

If you give your dog a bone, only to take it from him later, that's not fair, even in the context of teaching him how to be comfortable with human hands. That's a horrible exercise that only breeds anxiety in many under-socialized dogs, especially ones that had to scavenge for food. Instead, give him a size-appropriate bone, and leave him alone. Consider it your dog's version of "me time." If you are concerned that the bone is too small or dangerous, or that he has something he shouldn't have, it's important to work on "leave it" and "drop it" skills with lower value objects and increase the level of difficulty over time so you can eventually ask your dog to "drop it" in reference to something amazing, like a bone. Melissa Millet, Victoria Stilwell, and other positive reinforcement trainers have wonderful how-to videos online that demonstrate step-by-step how to teach "leave it" and "drop it" successfully.

If you just take things from your dog, or approach a dog that is growling for whatever reason, you are telling the dog that no matter what, its discomfort is of no consequence to you. It's better to pick your battles. If the dog is growling over a bone, especially one you gave him, *c'est la vie*. Change your thinking and just let him have something you gave him without threatening to take it away. On the other hand, if your dog is growling when people come into the home, won't drop things on command, or growls at the vet who's trying to draw blood for his overall health, this is an area where you need to get help, stat.

What are signs of dogs that were under-socialized?

In earlier chapters I discussed why it's important to seek ethical places to get a dog, and never pick one up off a truck. This is why that is so important. Many of these dogs, even at 12-weeks-old, have not only missed the bulk of the critical socialization period, but are also are high-drive dogs coming from remote areas known for hunting, tracking, and sporting. If you take high-drive dogs that are designed to hunt, put those traits into dogs that are born without people nearby, and put those dogs on a truck to be adopted in big cities, things can go wrong, quickly.

By taking dogs that have had no practical experience when it comes to surviving in an urban environment, and putting them on a truck with dozens of other dogs—who are barking, releasing stress hormones, and are scared—it's very likely that they have learned several important lessons. Dogs are scary. Trucks are scary. Crates are scary. When the door opens, and they see people waiting for them, people are scary.

We like to think that our dogs were born to love us. Over time trust can build to the point we can maybe call their affection for us "love," but that instant feeling of "Oh boy! That's my dog! I love her!" is not instantly reciprocated by many dogs that are coming off trucks and being homed in our cities. They are just doing the best they can to survive and cope, and often it takes weeks to months before problem behaviors start to show.

Under-socialized dogs tend to cower, maybe shake in the corner, seem tense, or look away often. They give off very "small" body language. They might even bark, appear aggressive at things that are scary to them, or try to get away. This is all normal in an under-socialized dog, but it needs attention. If you were afraid of something, you would either give off very clear body language that you dislike the situation you are in, or you would run. When I see a spider, I get tense, I stare at it, and I freeze. Dogs do this, too, when they see things they are unsure of or are outright afraid of.

Body Language 101

I'm going to start this by proclaiming that not every dog that wags his tail is happy. There, I've said it. Do you hear that? That's the sound of thousands of dog trainers sighing in unison. I have gone into dozens of homes where the owners emphatically state that Buddy was wagging his tail just before he bit a human. A wagging tail does not indicate that your dog is happy. How was the tail wagging? What was the rest of the dog's body language suggesting? What events occurred prior to the incident?

It's critical to take the entire body into account when decoding dog body language. A dog that has his hackles up is excited—but is he "good" excited (playing with his best friend) or is he "bad" excited (another dog is trying to take his favorite ball). Just like erect hackles don't necessarily indicate whether your dog is happy or upset, a wagging tail is not the sole indicator of "happiness" in your dog.

When I'm looking at a dog, I am looking for a series of telltale signs. Let me start at the ears: are they forward or back? When Sadie greeted me, she would whimper, she would get low and her ears would pull back; however, her eyes and face were soft. Her body was wiggly. If you take a different vocalization (a low growl), ears back, and a tense body, that is a dog that is posturing in defense, or even ready to strike. Sadie's ears were back when she greeted me, but the rest of her body told me everything I needed to know about how our interaction would go: she was preparing for our greeting ritual of rubbing up against my legs, and then "phwump" onto her back for a belly rub. Context matters, greatly.

Another arena where there is a need for more education is in the way that humans interact on a social level with dogs. Pet professionals have been saying for years that dogs don't love to be hugged (though, in the interest of full disclosure, I hugged Sadie all the time). More people need to understand that "hugging" is a primate behavior, not a canid behavior, and most dogs really don't like it. There are dogs (mine included) that were hugged every day. If you look at photos of that behavior, I look thrilled, and the dog looks annoyed—like a teenager who was asked to pose with her totally not-awesome parents for the holiday card.

Look at Sadie's face. What is it really saying?
Now, look at mine.
"Who is this hug really for?"
-The Incomparable Patricia McConnell, Ph.D.

Sadie learned to tolerate my primate behavior. She tolerated hugging from her family. Do you think she should tolerate the same behavior from a stranger? Would you tolerate such behavior from some dude on the train?

Now think about kids. Toddlers specifically, tend to hurl themselves at dogs. I had a relationship built on trust for over a decade with this particular dog. She tolerated me, and she knew that she would get a good payout for it, like a cookie. But when dogs get assaulted by small children, who only want to hug them, that's where problems arise. Dogs might "whap" their tail against the floor while turning their head away (as Sadie was starting to do in the above photo). We call the head turn avoidance behavior and the tail thump an appeasement gesture. Now look at that "whap" or "thump, thump, thump" of a tail, as a kid quickly closes the distance and the dog can't get away.

161

The dog gets annoyed because in dog-language, when someone rushes in on personal space it's considered a threatening behavior. For people, it is too. If someone charged me while I was sitting on the train, no matter what his motive, I would feel incredibly threatened by it.

Not all animals love to be hugged.
This is my younger brother with me, before we had a dog sledding team to play with.
If he were a dog, I'd deserve to get bitten. Thankfully, Matty didn't have teeth yet.
Unrelated: why didn't my parents foster my clearly natural martial arts talents?

Now, if that particular dog in the hypothetical example above ends up biting the child, it would very likely be to the face, because think about where faces go when hugs happen. For reference, see where my face is in both photos above. All the "hug-victim" has to do is turn his head and put teeth on my accessible cheek. Kids also have incredibly delicate skin, so if they get bitten, it tends to be worse than when an adult gets bitten, or another dog, who has thicker skin and a fur coat for protection.

When a specialist goes into the home to assess what happened, the owners are likely to report that "Buddy was wagging his tail just before he bit! The attack came out of nowhere!" Generally, after cases in which a kid was bitten, the focus of the family is on the intention of the child, which is totally understandable. "He just wanted to say hi and play with the dog!" Very rarely in a training appointment does anyone ever say, "I don't think the dog wanted to say hi."

I don't think Buddy understands the concept of intention, which is really what's happening. The kid intended to give the dog a nice hug, because that's what people do. The dog did not get that at all. The dog saw a threat, fast, squealing, and enthusiastic; a threat that didn't respond to subtler appeasement and avoidance cues like a head turn, a lip-lick or the tail flutter, and the adults in the room, in this hypothetical situation, didn't get the cues, either. To the untrained eye, it looks like the dog was wagging its tail just before biting a kid…out of nowhere. This hypothetical happens with more frequency than anyone would like.

Trainers and behavior specialists look at the whole picture: the ears, the eyes, the muzzle, the overall body posture, and the tail. We also look at events surrounding an incident or potential incident. If there is a paw lifted up in the air and the dog is physically tense while staring intensely at his handler, that is a dog that is likely concerned. This dog is making a decision to stay or run while looking for feedback from his owner. "Do I sit here? Do I bark? What do I do?" If the body is stiff and the tail is twitching behind an otherwise tense body, that is a dog looking for space and a dog that may not growl (see above) to indicate his frustration. Don't stare at this dog and don't approach. Think of it from the dog's perspective, not yours, no matter how much you "just want to say hi," or how much the kid just wants to hug the nice, fluffy dog.

Without offering any background on the photo below, what do you think this dog is saying?

*

This is Georgia. She had a litter of puppies, sat in a cage for two weeks in the South, and was spayed before her journey north. She's a dog that had just come off a truck and spent an entire week staring at walls just so she could cope. She couldn't look at people. She couldn't do anything. She was completely, totally, 100% terrified. Notice that her ears are pinned back, she's tucked into a space that fits around her body. Her tail is tucked in. She's not trying to be small. She's trying to be invisible. You don't need to be an expert in dog body language to know exactly what this dog is trying to say. "Stay away. I don't want any part of this. Please leave me alone. I mean you no harm."

Dogs will often lick their lips when they're nervous, yawn, or sniff the ground as a means of saying "Oh, jeez, would you look at the time! I have this thing I have to do....over there!" These are signals that your dog would rather have some space or not be present in the current situation, but she is willing to direct her attention to something totally different as a coping mechanism.

Renowned author and animal expert, Turid Rugaas, wrote a fantastic book on these subtle cues that we tend to ignore in our dogs—cues that dogs give us long before a growl ever happens or a bite occurs. She successfully argues that by paying attention to these cues, we can avoid a lot of problem behaviors like leash aggression or dog reactivity, two issues that are way too common in our cities. Instead of rehashing what Ms. Rugaas has so elegantly penned, I want to bring your attention to her book *On Talking Terms with Dogs: Calming Signals*. Read it, and you'll be a much better dog handler.

While you're at it, pick up Patricia McConnell's *The Other End of the Leash*, which is a great read I recommend to all of my students. It's arguably the most important book I've ever read about living life with dogs.

Thanks to my friend Robyn Townsend for sharing Georgia's story and photo. Georgia was adopted by Britany Merrick, an amazing soul who did wonders with Georgia. She's done well with lots of patience, care, a family-of-one, and is learning to trust. One person, the RIGHT person, can make a world of difference. Georgia would have likely failed in a big urban center, or a family with small children running around all day long. This match worked out and illustrates the importance of knowing the dog and knowing where she will likely succeed.

The Multi-Pet Household

Two dogs are better than one! Right?

Whether you're introducing another dog, a cat, multiple cats, rabbits, or more exotic critters like lizards, there are ways to introduce everyone for optimal success. It's important to remember that each species needs specific arrangements in order to be satisfied. Additionally, each animal has a unique personality, so though they have general needs that have to be met, there may be additional requirements for each pet in the home.

In this chapter I explore specifically multiple-dog households, as well as dog and cat households. However, looking at these dynamics should help you determine what to do for other animals that may be introduced to your home, no matter how exotic.*

*Advice not applicable to tigers. Please stay within the realm of portable and legal creatures for the purposes of this discussion.

"My Dog Needs A Buddy!" What to Consider When Adding Another Dog to the Home:

First, consider why you are looking to add another dog to your home. If you are gone all day and don't have enough time to dedicate to your existing dog, it would be completely unfair to both dogs to enlist the buddy system. If you are looking to get a second dog primarily so your dog can get exercise, it's not fair and your neighbors would hate you. It's your job to exercise your dog, not another dog's burden. It's also important to note that problem behaviors tend to get worse in the company of other dogs, not better, so be sure that all issues are fixed and managed comfortably, and you have a routine that satisfies the needs of the existing pets in the home before bringing another critter into the fold.

If you have a dog that's pretty balanced, genuinely enjoys the company of other dogs, and adding another dog to your family is something everyone wants, then go for it! Follow the suggestions in previous chapters and do a lot of research. This time, it's important to find a dog that will also fit into your environment, fit your lifestyle, and love other dogs, most specifically your existing dog. The usual recommendation from trainers is to find a dog of the opposite sex, though I know many successful placements with dogs of the same gender. The new prospect should have similar energy level or lower energy. You don't ever want to add a dog of higher energy to the family, because that tends to backfire and becomes overwhelming for the resident dog. The goal is to find a dog that makes your current dog comfortable, which should prevent a lot of problems down the road.

When most people are thinking about adding another dog, the general idea is that it's not much more work to take two dogs for a walk, feed two dogs, and carry on in the same way that you had with one dog. While that is the ideal, it takes a lot of work to get to that point. Some families never quite get that far. What tends to happen is one dog starts to bark on walks so the other chimes in, or one dog starts resource guarding toys and the other doesn't understand why he can't have his favorite ball. They can even start to ignore basic foundational commands in favor of wrestling with their new playmate.

The number one recommendation I give to multi-dog households is to make certain that a few times a week at minimum, each dog gets time with the humans in the home, without the other dog present. This is important for many reasons:

- **Training:** It's easier to train a dog when there are fewer distractions, including the distractions of other pets in the home. Whether you are teaching new tricks or brushing up on old skills, it's important to set your dog up for success. Teaching two dogs not to exuberantly leap at the door when company shows up is as close to setting dogs up to fail as you can get. Instead, work with one dog at a time. Once both dogs have the behavior you want individually, work with them both present.
- **Relationships:** Dogs build new relationships with each person in the home individually, and each resident pet individually. The best way to build these relationships and increase the likelihood of each dog listening to commands, is to work for just a few minutes each day with each dog one-on-one.
- **Breaks:** Just like people need breaks from other people from time to time, including loved ones, dogs need breaks from other resident dogs. This is especially true in the city, since they are already bombarded with stimuli every minute of every day. Take one dog to a fun agility class, while leaving the other dog at home with a special treat, or give each dog his own 20 minute sniffy walk. Find unique ways to build the relationship between you and each dog in the home.
- **Emergency Care:** When the dogs are used to being apart from

each other for periods of time, it's easier to cope if something were to happen. Imagine one dog gets sick and has to stay overnight in the hospital. How would each dog tolerate being left behind by his buddy overnight? It might be a tough night, but it's better if they're used to spending some time alone from day one, instead of only when things go wrong.

Different Strokes for Different (Doggie) Folks:

Sometimes our dogs have different individual needs. I've mentioned how Sadie and Zeppelin needed different overnight care considerations, because their tolerance level for specific things were on opposite sides of the spectrum. Zeppy could stay with other dogs, and loved it. Sadie hated the idea of any other dog in her space aside from Zeppy, so having her stay with friends who had dogs was unfair to everyone. Exercise was a similar consideration: Zeppy could go to the dog park and really enjoyed zooming with other dogs, whereas it stressed Sadie out to no end to have a flock of dogs she couldn't herd. Sadie could go off leash in fields, and Zep couldn't be trusted off leash. For a while, we had to walk each dog separately to teach them each how to focus on a handler on walks instead of revving up and barking at passing dogs on their morning constitutional.

When there are two dogs in a home, the work is often exponentially higher, because each dog might have different needs. If you have the time, the patience, and the ability to work with each dog individually as well as together, having a second dog in a home can be very rewarding. Your dog has a playmate, companion, and another of the same species under the same roof. I always got such great joy knowing my relationship with each dog was different. Zep was our cuddle bug before he passed away. He was our 80 pound lapdog that was even keel and loved car rides. Sadie was our working dog that didn't know how to relax, but I had years of fun competing with her in canine disc. When she was older, she loved to go on walks, and though she was still intense, she was teaching our interns at NEDTC how to be effective trainers by handling a predictably reactive dog in an appropriate way. Zeppy couldn't come to classes, and Sadie didn't cuddle. Each dog was very different, and each touched a different part of our hearts. With those differences came a lot more work on our part, structuring different activities to keep them each happy individually, but we did it because we loved our dogs. In return they were able to live peaceably together, for the most part, for six years.

Don't assume that each dog you bring into your home will love being with other dogs, or that your dog that loves other dogs would adore a permanent companion. To test the waters, borrow a friend's dog for a few nights, or when your neighbors go on vacation, volunteer to take their well-adjusted dog. Is there any resource guarding? How can you manage any potential resource-guarding issues in a small space? Are there any problems on leash when two dogs are walking in the city instead of one? Is one dog barking, and the other chiming in? What happens when you leave two dogs alone when you go to work? Have the neighbors called Animal Control for incessant barking, or is all quiet on the Western front? These are all things that are better to know in advance, so you aren't totally caught off guard. Some dogs that adore the company of other dogs might not do so well with the company of dogs long term, so you are best to find out before you sign paperwork on a permanent bro-dog for your pup.

My suggestion to anyone looking for a second dog is simple: Plan on doing each activity during the day separately, and if they can be walked together or go to the park together, that's a bonus. Don't plan on being able to do every activity with both dogs together, because you might end up disappointed, or force one of the dogs into something that makes him uncomfortable, which leads to unnecessary stress for everyone.

Dog to Cat Introductions/Debunking the Cat Myths for Dog People:

Cuddle Buddies: Rohan the cat and Zeppelin the dog. This was Rohan's favorite spot for six years. Zeppy was less than enthusiastic with this relationship, but he was too lazy to move.

Cats' needs are very different from dogs'. For starters, cats must have access to high spaces in order to feel safe and also have access to dark hidey-holes to duck into. Cat-shelves are a big hit for the cats in our homestead, but if you don't want to spend several hundred dollars on special shelves for your cats, you can do what we did: Go to your local hardware store and get some nice, sturdy shelves that you like for $7.00 each. Affix some carpet remnants to them so the cats don't slide off when they jump up, and then stagger them so they can get to varying heights. Alternatively, see where they like to go and make it comfy. Our cats love the top of the cabinets in our kitchen. They jump up on top of the fridge, hop up to the top of the cabinets, and stay there all day long. It's cool in the summer, warm in the winter, and sunnier than any other part of our apartment. I put a couple of blankets and towels up there, as well as an old cardboard box that they sleep in. It doesn't have to be expensive, but it does have to be accessible and high, and most importantly, in a place that they'll enjoy. This is even more important when you have several animals on the food chain hierarchy living in one space together. Cats need varying heights and places to duck where they can feel safe from your dog. Pulling the sofa out by a few inches is also a good way to provide a little nook for cats only, assuming your cat is smaller than your dog.

If you are getting a new cat, consider keeping it in one room with food, water and a litter box for a few days so the pet can acclimate to a new environment and the people in the home first. If the dog is the new pet, keep the dog tethered to you for a couple of days, and make sure the cat has plenty of places to hide under, and climb on.

Every interaction needs to be actively supervised, at least until everything is running smoothly. Dogs and cats should be supervised in the beginning. Cats and cats should be supervised at the beginning. Dogs and dogs should be supervised at the beginning. 16-year-old teenagers should be supervised at the beginning. When not able to supervise, put the new animal in a designated room or space where she has the necessities— food, water, amusement, safety, and a litter box.

In addition to cat-shelves, the animals should have separate areas for food and elimination needs. For four years we had a designated cat room, which was our second bathroom. We were able to keep the dogs away from the cat food and away from the irresistible *kitty crunchies* (read: kitty poo) with the use of a baby gate. This also gave the cats an area that was just theirs if company came over, they weren't feeling social, or if the vacuum was running.

As always, your dog will need a reliable recall and needs to know the command *leave it*. There are great videos from Victoria Stilwell and Melissa Millett on YouTube, demonstrating what leave it actually should look like and how to teach it effectively. Hopefully, things won't deteriorate so you need a drop it command, but if you get that far, it's clear the dog was too amped up to handle the interaction. Use a leash on the dog when the pets are first introduced to keep both parties safe. Also, make sure that your dog has had plenty of physical exercise before any introductions.

Everyone worries about the dog attacking the cat, and they should, but cats have knives that come out of their feet and they can do some serious damage to a dog's muzzle, eyes, and human hands if you get in the way. The only time I was sent to the hospital from working with animals was when I decided to move a hissing cat instead of moving a 40 pound dog that was cornered by the aforementioned cat. I should have picked up the dog. I never saw what blood poisoning looked like until I was bitten by a nine-pound devil-cat and had to go to the emergency room.

Internet sensation Talented K9 Tonya and her friend, Duchess (the 3-Legged Wonder Cat) take a break from a day of hard work. Owner Sarah DeChamplain lives with her furry friends in Gainesville, GA. You can follow their adventures on YouTube or Google+.

Cats are also gregarious. It's a fallacy that you can leave them for days on end without human attention and they don't care. Yes, many cats are fine with food and water for a couple of days, but cats are highly social creatures. When they are neglected, they can develop behavior issues just like our dogs can. Don't get a cat just to keep your dog company or because you want a pet that can be ignored. Cats need exercise, attention, and they are very trainable. If you don't believe me, search YouTube for "cat tricks." They can do amazing things, but we don't tend to think of cats as able to do party tricks or tasks.

Cats also need to be indoors. Letting your domestic cat outside in the city is one of the more irresponsible things you can do. For starters, cats that live indoors can live well into their teens, and some into their early twenties, but cats that roam have an average lifespan of only four years or less in urban environments. They pick up parasites that can get transmitted back to the other pets or people in the home. They pick up diseases, get hit by cars, and become lost. Outdoor cats tend to mark if they are un-neutered. They meow, fight, and poop in neighboring yards, which isn't something that most neighbors enjoy. They also breed like rabbits. Do your cat a favor: If you decide to get a cat, keep it inside. There are plenty of ways to keep an indoor cat happy without irritating neighbors or risking an early death for the cat. Read anything by Ketenna Jones, cat behavior specialist, or Steve Dale if you want more information on cat behavior and integration.

Final Thoughts:

Your existing animals need honesty from you. It would be unfair to a highly prey-driven dog that chases everything to introduce a cat that will run and trigger a prey response in that dog. It would be equally unfair to introduce a new bouncy puppy to a household that has a 17-year-old cat who is afraid of absolutely everything and can't get away to safety fast enough. If you have a dog that can't tolerate other dogs, adding a second dog into the fold is perhaps not the best idea. Think about the animals you already have and ask if it would really be fair to integrate a new critter into the home. If you have a social dog that seems curious around cats, a well-trained dog that loves other dogs, or a cat that doesn't seem to care when there are visiting dogs over, then those might be excellent candidates for a multi-pet/multi-species household. If it's not the case, you still might be able to get another pet, but you really have to do your homework or consult a specialist to help with the integration.

For further information on how to conduct the introduction step by step, ASPCA.org has a fantastic resource section specifically dedicated to introducing dogs and cats, and Steve Dale has a blog, podcast, and several books on the matter. Just remember to go slowly, never punish your dog or cat for being fearful, and don't drag either party into an introduction. It's crucial that the introduction is going at the pace of the animals and everyone feels safe. Alternatively, you can call in a professional to help you get things started correctly.

If you do it right, and do your research, you can have a happy existence with a multi-pet household. However, you have to do it right, and you have to be fair to everyone who already lives in the home, including all the existing resident pets.

Temperature Considerations
Too cold? Too hot? Just right?

What's the deal with coats?:

A coat or jacket might be an appropriate option for dogs that live their lives in climate-controlled conditions. City dogs don't tend to live outside. As a result they don't adjust as well to the elements as their forefathers once did. There are some dogs that are more sensitive to the cold and should wear protection when venturing outside:

- Older dogs, especially those with arthritis and sore joints
- Dogs with very little body fat (like greyhounds, Boston terriers, and whippets)
- Chinese crested dogs (the naked dogs with a tuft of hair. Obviously.)
- Dogs that keep their fur coats short year-round to prevent matting should compensate for the shorter coat.

Murphy wears his coat to the dog park. He usually has a haircut year round to prevent matting. While he is mat-free, it can be difficult for him to stay warm on colder days. Plus, his owner, Som-Dog VP Jocelyn Fassett, can prevent a lot of that "wet-dog smell" by keeping him covered!

Seriously? Booties? For dogs?:

When you partner evolution (fur on the inside of the paw pads) and the insulating qualities of snow, most dogs will fair relatively well running through the woods after a snow fall. Some dog breeds are built for life in the snow, like Malamutes, huskies, and St. Bernards.

Concrete, however, is not insulating. It's brutal on paws. The exposed skin on the bottom of a dog's feet is incredibly sensitive to the bitter cold of sidewalks, streets and cobblestone. When you match cold concrete with rock salt (a common chemical used in cities to melt the snow), you have a recipe for painful paws, ice balls forming between the paw pads, and cuts due to salt – which get more painful because now the dog has salt in the wound. Literally.

Dogs can get frostbite on their paws. They have not evolved protection for concrete so we need to make sure that we're offering some sort of protection. Even the bulliest bully breed and the furriest arctic dogs have exposed skin on their paws that are no match for salt, chemicals, freezing slush that chills to the bone, and frozen concrete. So yes – booties for dogs. It's not just a weird thing city folk do. It's sensible and protective for our pets.

Can I just use 'mushers wax' instead of boots?

Mushers wax is a product that we used running our dog-sledding dogs. I see it sold in most pet stores in this area. It's certainly an option, but it doesn't protect dogs from everything. For starters, wax is used to prevent ice balls from forming in between paw pads, so unless your dog is running through the snow, it's not really doing what it's supposed to do. Secondly, the wax is no more of a barrier than lip balm for our chapped lips. It is a mild barrier and can be great, but it's not going to protect a dog from slush, the cold concrete or salt.

With that being said, wax might be an option for dogs that hate boots and only need a quick walk around the block. It's better than no protection at all. Just make sure to wipe all paws off when entering the home to get all the chemicals that might be stuck to the wax off the dogs' paws – you don't want Fido licking rock salt, or worse, off his feet while trying to remove the wax himself. Furthermore, you don't want this stuff tracked through your condo or apartment.

I live in warmer climates. When should I walk my dog?

Remember earlier I mentioned that pavement and concrete are not insulating? That same principle in physics applies to heat as well. If it's too hot for the back of your hand on the pavement, it's too hot for a dog's exposed paws. I used to wear Vibram® toe shoes when I walked dogs in the summer. They were not my favorite fashion statement, but I could feel the heat of the pavement through the barefoot technology. If it was too hot for me, it was too hot for the dogs in my care.

173

Whatever the climate, make sure your dog stays hydrated like
Capall, a Bouvier des Flandres. Owner Colleen Skeuse helps him get a drink on a warm day.

Additionally, there are dogs that can't handle the heat as well as other dogs. If your dog is refusing to walk, it might be too hot, or he might be uncomfortable. Don't make him "tough-it-out." Here is an incomplete list of dogs that are more susceptible to skyrocketing temperatures:

- Brachycephalic breeds (pugs, bulldogs, Boston terriers, Pekingese, and other dogs with a smooshed-in face).
- Greyhounds and other breeds that have very little body fat. As a result, they cannot insulate against the cold or heat very well.
- Heavy coated dogs such as (but not limited to) malamutes, huskies, Samoyeds, and Australian shepherds
- Small dogs are way more susceptible to temperatures than their medium sized counterparts. This is because as heat reflects off of the pavement, it reflects up to more surface area, heating up the underbelly of smaller dogs. Bigger dogs are further from the reflective surface, so are safer in that regard to overheating.
- Older dogs can't regulate their temperatures as easily as younger dogs, so caution must be taken with this population.
- Puppies often don't know when to quit playing, even when it's hot outside. They will continue to run around, even as signs of heat stroke start to occur. Watch puppies and high energy dogs closely.

That fuzzy lump on Alan Torpey's back is his 65 pound Australian shepherd, Roger. Alan carried his buddy over the North Bank Bridge on a sweltering summer day because Roger's feet were burning on the concrete. Hot days are hard for our furry friends, but we do what we can to make them comfortable. Good boy, Alan.

Saying Goodbye
Considerations for end-of-life

Even unemployed dogs have a job to do—and that job is enriching our lives. If that's the definition of work, they go their entire existence working for us. Unfortunately, their job is done far too soon. Whether it's eight years and nine months, or eleven years and six months, it's always too soon.

After they leave us, there is the debate of whether or not to get a new dog, how long to wait, and other questions. Everyone has an answer, but the answer is solely dependent on the person in question. The relationship with the previous dog is absolutely a factor.

My dad swore he'd never get another dog after the last of his dog sledding team passed away, though the entire family knew it was a matter of time before he'd be out with another canine companion. It took my father four years before he was ready to invest his soul into another buddy. The right one came around at the shelter where he volunteered, and that dog is still always by his side. It was a decision he had to make, when the time was right and the dog was right. In hindsight, I'm glad he waited because his 90 pound mush-of-a-dog, Sushi, is the perfect dog for him. Sushi is no indication that Dad loved his other dogs any less. Each dog is a different relationship entirely. We kept pressuring him to get a dog, but he wasn't ready. We were wrong to pressure him, and he was right to wait.

Our dogs can leave suddenly, or they can depart after a long, slow illness, but this is true: they will all eventually leave. The degree of pain is an indicator as to how much our lives are really, truly affected by the dogs we love. If it hurts like hell, that means they did their job well.

Even though they were both euthanized, there are many differences between the decisions we made as a family for our two dogs. There are also differences in how we said farewell to them as individuals. If you are dealing with this stage of life, you are not alone.

Led Zeppelin, CGC (12/2/2004 - 9/2/2013)

Led Zeppelin, or "Zeppy," our greyhound, passed away on Labor Day, 2013. He was a big, black dog—get it? If you don't, just Google it. It's ok. I'll wait...

He was just shy of nine years old when we had to make a really tough decision—arguably the first really tough decision of my then seven-year partnership with my husband. It's hard to put into words the first time you have the opportunity, and responsibility, of giving your friend the last gift

176

you can give him; the gift of taking away his pain.

Zeppy jumped off of the couch to greet us when we got back from celebrating Labor Day with friends. When he jumped off the couch, I heard a crack, and saw his leg was broken. It was then that I knew that Zep was going to Angell Memorial Hospital in Boston and not coming home. My husband did not come to the realization that this was it for his best friend, and I just couldn't tell him.

I am not a vet, as I say often in my blog, in appointments and in this book, but I worked with a lovely woman who adopted many greyhounds over my time knowing her. She should be the Patron Saint of Greyhounds, because she adopted older greys, loved them often for a just a short while, until they would get bone cancer and pass on. It broke her heart every time, because she loved those dogs with every ounce of her being. When we got Zeppelin, I knew we'd be saying goodbye in a similar fashion. We just thought it would be later.

When it's your dog, you always think it's "later".

Sip drove my husband and Zeppy to the hospital, and I met them after I fed our baby at home. I wanted them to say "Nope, lucky for you this is just Clumsy Greyhound Syndrome. He's patched up and ready to go!" But the clinical signs were there. I just knew, and I never in my life wanted to be so wrong.

We went into the room where Zeppy got to hang out with us. He was in so much pain, his leg was the size of a linebacker's, but he still tried his best to limp over to us. We laid him down on a blanket, the Emergency Vet met us in the room, and Zep put his head in my lap. My husband talked to him, petted his head and shoulder while the medication started to numb his pain. I looked into his eyes, and saw relief.

Often, we put human terms and feelings onto our dogs. I know what I saw, and I saw an animal who wasn't hurting for the last minute of his life. He looked at me, he sighed a big sigh, laid his head on my lap, and fell asleep.

There is no way to ask our pets if they want to go on living, or if they prefer us to end their suffering. We can't ask them, "Hey, you have maybe six months to a year to live, but we have to take your leg. What do you think?" We can only do our best, as we always do the best for our animals. We might not be able to give them the best quality food, but we can give them the best we can afford. We might not be able to let them off leash, but we can find ways to let them be dogs. We might make them live indoors instead of rolling in the dirt, but we find ways to enrich their lives, and in return for that, all we ask of them is loyalty, affection, and sad puppy dog eyes. They keep our feet warm, and our houses safe from intruders. They give us funny stories, and occasional stains on the carpet (or in Zeppy's case, the fake Christmas tree, because he thought that meant he had indoor privileges).

They give us an opportunity to connect, to be responsible for something else, and to be more human. In Zep's case, he taught me how to take a chill-pill and relax, something humans have been trying to teach this Type A individual for decades to no avail.

I have no idea what Zeppelin would have wanted, but I do not regret the decision we made. I think back to the horrible sound of his bones cracking, his howling, and his uncontrollable panting—and then I think of his head relaxing, his eyes looking directly into mine, and a sigh of relief. We made that decision for Zep, and I'm not sure I'd make it for every dog we have, but I do think it was the right call for him.

That doesn't mean it's an easy call, and it doesn't mean it's the right call for every dog. But for him, for us, and for the facts on the table, we did what we thought was right.

We did the best we could, Buddy. We did the best we could.

This photo of Zeppelin was taken by my dear friend Dan Maher.
As a stained glass artist in Cambridge, Dan has an eye for capturing a great
moment in time.

Rest in peace, Zep. And keep an eye on my friends Samwise, Dennis, and Paul. Sam is the spaniel who thinks he's a Border collie. Dennis and Paul are probably jamming on guitars and pianos by the fireplace. They 'get' dogs, and I think you'll do well to stay with them.

Sadie-Jane Dogg, CGC (Approximately 12/28/2003 - 8/27/2014)

During the process of sending this book to the editor, my beloved companion and faithful friend of nearly twelve years was put to sleep on the same weekend, one year after greyhound. One year, two dogs, and the same holiday weekend seems a bit unfair, but that's how it goes sometimes. The house is remarkably quiet, even with a toddler running through it, because our dogs are no longer a part of the household.

The cats, however, seem much happier.

For Zeppy, the decision was clear. He had bone cancer and he was in pain. For Sadie, the right thing was less clear, which made the decision much more difficult in some ways, and much easier in others.

When dogs age, functions start to decline. Cognitively, our dogs may be different from when they were younger. As Sadie aged, she became like the quintessential crotchety old lady on the front steps. If she had a shotgun (and thumbs), she would yell at everyone to get off her lawn. When she was working at New England Dog Training Club with our intern Carl, or walking with the family, she was happy. When she was playing disc, she was happy but clearly very, very sore. When she couldn't do those things over the summer, due to heat and her old-lady body, she declined behaviorally, cognitively, and physically.

There comes a point when the behavior modification medication might not work anymore, and it's kinder to say goodbye. Yes, we could have upped her medication, but to what degree of her happiness? She was miserable not being able to work and run for more than three minutes before coming up lame or exhausted, but that seemed to me like a terrible reason to put down a friend.

When her cognition started to fade and she didn't know what a ball was, or she barked in the corner at night for no obvious reason, they were just written off as goofy quirks for an older dog that still had a lot of life left.

When she got up suddenly to play with my daughter, but was in so much pain physically, and also may have had a cognitive slip, that she knocked the baby down and bit her in the face, the decision was made for us. It was then that we knew it was time to say goodbye, before anyone got more seriously hurt. It was then that we knew Sadie was telling us she had had enough, and maybe she was telling us she was done.

We could have kept her managed in the kitchen as long as the baby was awake, but to relegate Sadie, the most human-social dog I've ever known, to the kitchen would have been torture for her and for me. We could have upped her medication so she'd sleep and cope, but after a dozen years, she deserved more than that. Like Zeppelin, we could have kept her alive, but it wouldn't be fair to our dog, and since our toddler was at risk of further injury it was a no brainer for me, though regrettable that the incident even happened.

I had a couple people ask if I could have re-homed her. If she were a three year old dog, loved everything about life and could go to a great home in the country to play ball all day, then yes. When the dog in question is almost at the end of her statistical natural life, who is clearly a dog that is bonded to one family, is on expensive behavior modification medication, has tumors on her back, blown out knees, vision problems, arthritis in joints I didn't even know dogs had, is dog aggressive, is cognitively failing, and starting to aggress in ways that are atypical for this particular dog, then I would say the answer is clearly no. Some people might still say yes, re-home her. I couldn't do that to her, I couldn't put that cost and management burden on another family, and if I'm being 100% honest, I couldn't cope with her living out her days with someone else.

I have met with families and have had to say, "You should send this dog back to the shelter, because he's aggressive to kids, and you have kids in and out of this house all day long. This is a mismatch; let's give you and your family a better shot at of having a true companion, while giving this dog a shot of finding a home better suited for him."

Let me be perfectly clear: Dog trainers do not *like* to say this to anyone. We want it to work as much as you do. However, it's our job to look at the well-being of the family and the dog, use our expertise, and sometimes suggest what an owner might think is the unthinkable. These tend to be younger dogs that still have a chance at a good life, but will not likely cut it in the city or with a particular family. Every dog is an individual, and every dog deserves the best shot of being successful. Sometimes that means it's not with a particular family, and that's o.k. You didn't fail if you tried everything and it didn't work out. Relationships are *hard*. Especially considering that this relationship is bilingual.

In ten years, I have had to tell three clients that the kindest thing to do was to euthanize the dog. Those were the three hardest cases I've ever worked, but I went home after those appointments knowing I gave them the best advice I could for their particular situation. It's not easy, but if I had a student in my situation, passing the buck to have someone else put Sadie to sleep in the likely near-future would not have been fair to the other family, and I would have been worried sick that she was not being treated with dignity, compassion, and fairness in her aging years. The buck with

Sadie stopped with me, her owner, her partner, her love. I owed her that much.

Had we lived in the country with a field and didn't have a kid, then she may have made it another two years or more. If Aislyn came along two or three years earlier, Sadie might have felt better and they may have been buddies for the rest of Sadie's life. Was her life full with us in the city? I can't ask her, but I would like to think so. It was harder in many ways to live in the city with a Border collie, with this particular Border collie, but I had to think outside of the box, which made things more interesting for both of us, and I wouldn't have had it any other way.

The dogs we get when we're younger change and evolve, just like we do. I'm not the same person I was at 22 when I got her out of a shelter (which I'm sure my husband is thankful for), and she wasn't the same dog I picked out of the Franklin County Animal Shelter, though we were fundamentally similar to those two creatures who met on opposing sides of a metal cage. She sat in a crawlspace of my Chevy S-10, just eight months into our relationship, when we moved from Ohio to Maine, and shortly after, from Maine to Boston. She was always in the passenger's seat of my little S-10, and when I got a more appropriate vehicle, one that didn't beg people to ask me to help them move every weekend, she moved to the back seat where things were safer for her, but she was always there. My copilot. My buddy.

Our journey was long, spirited, enjoyable, and I am ever thankful for all that came out of my life with her. She didn't get me hired by a dog trainer on-the-spot in 2004, but she did need an activity, which got me involved in canine disc, where that dog trainer happened to see me working with future disc dogs. He liked the cut of my jib, so I was hired as a dog trainer without any qualifications. I worked hard to earn my certification and to work in this industry that I love so much.

Sadie didn't make my relationship with Brian, but she was cute enough to get his attention, and I had to do the rest.

I didn't get into dog training to get into behavior work, but the deck of cards fell that way when I found myself in the same shoes many of my now students find themselves in. I know what they are feeling and understand the ethics of keeping dogs that need an around-the-clock management plan.

Sadie at Dogtown – an abandoned stone cutters' village near Gloucester, MA.
This photo sums up the relationship with my departed friend quite perfectly.
This photo sums up many people's relationship with their dogs quite perfectly.
It is a hard road for many of these relationships, but at the core is loyalty, and love.

Rest in peace, my dear friend Sadie. I knew I'd have to write this someday, but that didn't mean that I ever wanted to. I'm so, so, so sorry for so many things (the prong collars, the busy city life that you couldn't quite adjust to, and not listening, because I'm a dumb human who didn't get dog body language, despite being around dogs my whole life). Part of me wishes I had stayed in the country with you instead of moving to Boston, but I don't think either of us would have been at our happiest, and look at what we both would have missed out on. City life was a struggle for us both. We managed, but I still wish I could have done more for you, Pup. I wish I knew more at the beginning, and I wish that I could have given you a yard to hang out in at the end.

A few people said, "You two were such a great team." I couldn't have said it better. You were joy in motion, and I thank you for spending your time with me and choosing me as your person. I promise to take everything I learned with you, write a book (here it is!) and really listen to what all of our future dogs tell us. I promise to be honest with my students about what their dogs need, and to do so compassionately. I promise never to forget you. You were my longest relationship so far, and I thank you for every single minute of that time.

For the record, Sadie, more people have said they missed you, they loved you, or they were sorry for your passing than spoke of the birth of Aislyn or my wedding. You really, really, truly were one of a kind, and I knew it. I miss you.

The last photo my husband took of Sadie, two weeks before she died. It was taken on film, not digitally. Before her death, it became my favorite photo of her. The way the light hit her, made her glow ethereally. She looked happier and younger than she did at any point in her last year with us. It now has much more meaning.

Acknowledgements

I need to first thank my ever-supporting husband, Brian. Seriously, I wouldn't have been able to do all the things I wanted to do in the last eight years without your support and love. You stayed in the nine-to-five world so I could get my training certification. I often worked nights and weekends. There were times we went several days without seeing each other. You did so with no (um...minimal) complaint. There are no words for that freedom, responsibility, or affection. You were also the last set of eyes on this because I knew you would make sure it was perfect. I love you.

To my daughter, Aislyn: Well, I'd be lying if you weren't affected by my line of work. You chewed on Kong toys when you were teething, and you stole Sadie's kennel because you wanted new sleeping quarters. Some people told me kids were just like dogs—kids are not dogs. Dogs are not kids. Though, some of the techniques applied in my world did work remarkably well for you.

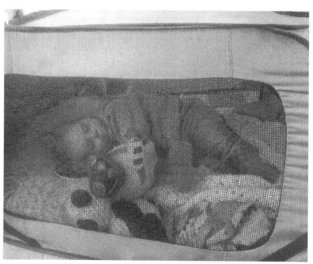

Aislyn, asleep in her "fort"—a dog crate.
My two-year-old is effectively crate trained.

Since this was a self-published adventure, I roped in several folks in to make sure the information was correct and accurate from a scientific and professional perspective. Veterinarian and bestie, Dr. Sip Siperstein; dog trainer, friend and gin aficionado, Leah Tremble, CPDT-KA; shelter goddess and dog trainer, Kim Melanson; dog care provider and play-group supervisor, Pat Dains; President of New England Dog Training Club, Jessica Fry, KPA-CTP; Grooming Guru, Alison MacDonald; and Dr. Laurie Siperstein-Cook at the SPCA in Sacramento: Thank you from the bottom of my little heart for making sure the information was as accurate as it could be as of the date of this writing, that the book was enjoyable, and for encouraging me to put this out into the wild. Your support and critiques made a huge difference and I can't thank you enough.

A very special thank you goes to Judith Kurtz Bogdanove and Ken Mallon for editing this entire piece from a writing perspective. You didn't have to fact check anything (I left that to the above pet professionals!), so you could just focus on grammar. Without you, I wouldn't have figured out the very interesting difference between *bad ass tattoos*, and *badass tattoos*. (Think about it, they are very, very different.) I feel that having you professionals edit this to ensure that it was readable and sound really made me feel like I was in a position to put this out in order to help dog owners navigate life with their pets, which is something we can all support.

Dad—why on earth you thought it was a "good idea" to take on ten dogs after your buddy Jack left them with you after running the Iditarod is beyond me. Oddly, it seemed to work out and I learned a lot about what to do, what not to do and how to be present with animals because of those dogs. I'm sorry about being a teenager, but it all worked out in the end. Go Pats!

To Melissa Mullen of Melissa Mullen Photography—thank you for donating such wonderful photos of shelter dogs, as well as donating your professional work for this piece. Thank you for being so generous with your work!

To Emily Sterne of Emily Sterne Photography – thank you as well for letting me repurpose the spectacular wedding photos you took of Brian and me, and use them for this book. I think they made a world of difference here, and I thank you for being so generous with your photographs.

Thank you also to all of the dog owners, students, and blog followers who provided photos of your dogs. I wrote about relationship-based, science-based dog training – but without these photos and your stories, these are just words on a page, or a screen. What you added in the last moments before publishing made this book a million times better – thank you for sharing your dogs with everyone. I hope you enjoy the book.

Tom & Lynn McGrath; Elizabeth McGrath & Dale Kocevski; Heather Marie McCue; Matthew 'Bud' McCue; Mom; Kelly Tozier McCue; Matthew I. Rasmussen (Razz!); Lindsay LeClair & Dan Miller (and Little Calvin!); Jon, Judy and Kal-El Bogdanove; Bogland; The Martucci's; Sarah Rose

Miller; Maura Kennedy & Steve Turcott; Adam Garland & Danielle McCarthy; Kate Tanski (and by extension, Ben!); Eva Kopf-Ridout & Matt Ridout; Shira & Leo Dragun; Tom Heath; The Blazeks, Elizabeth Bianchi; Colin Sutch; The Kopishke Family; Justin Handfield; The Moss family; Devon Perry and Family; You're not dog folk per-se, but you are people folk, and I love you for it. Thank you, to all of you—I'm blessed to have such an amazing, extended family.

To "Chuck," the damned horse that bucked me off two months into my collegiate career: I don't even know if you're still alive (probably not) but your breaking my spine was one of the best things that happened. Because of your ability to toss insecure equine science majors to the ground, coupled with my being too lazy to transfer out of Lake Erie College, I was fortunate enough to finish a degree in Psychology headed by Dr. Stephen Yachanin and Dr. James Eisenberg. With more than a little help from Dr. Dennis McDermot, Paul Gothard III and his wife, Sunni Gothard, I was able to get a degree in science instead of art and graduate with honors. I also learned in a class at LEC how to commit arson effectively, which is a skill I haven't finely tuned but the lesson plan stuck. Thanks to all of you for making learning theory fun and showing me how to be a teacher. I use those skills every single day, which is something that more people should be able to say about their college degree.

And of course, to the dog folk: April Terrio-Manning, Animal Control Officer of Somerville, Massachusetts; Janet Vera CPDT-KA; Diane Kurkjian, CPDT-KA; my partner-in-crime, Donna Culbert, CPDT-KA; Nancy "the Collie lady" Thompson; Vivian Zottola, CPDT-KA; all of the trainers at NEDTC; Liz Shaw of Far Fetched Farm in NH; Michelle Fournier and "Harry" at Durty Harry's; Riverdog; Dylis Burke; Carl James; Jordan Clements; Justin Aucoin and Kate Sokol; Pat and Jaron, owners of On The Run Boston; Dr. Sip and Doug Berman; Dan Maher; Sarah "The Patron Saint of Greyhounds" Norton; Dr. Samantha Simonelli, DVM; Dr. Sue Gilmore, DVM; Dr. Astrid Kruse, DVM; Everyone at VCA Wakefield Represent!; Brian Davis, Jocelyn Fassett and the entire Som|Dog organization; Marjie Alonso, CDBC, CPDT-KA, KPA-CTP, CTP; Gordon Fontaine, CTC; the Yankee Flyers Dog and Disc Club; and the Beantown Disc Dog Club: I have you here because you took a chance on me, taught me something invaluable, made me laugh at something in class, let me be your teacher, or said, "It's ok. You got this," at some point in my career. Even if we don't get on anymore, it's important to recognize that something you said had a positive impact and helped create this. Or you are just awesome and didn't mind that my white dog loved to rub against your black pants.

A shout-out to a few of the best dogs I've had the opportunity to know (and the families who love them): Ollie StaHartke, the Flying Boston Terrier; "Badger" Bandito Bandit Kennedy-Turcott; Bacchus; Stanley; Pip; Shale; Roger; Remy; Emma; Lola; Hera (RIP); Ashleigh (RIP); Pepper (RIP); Charlie Murray; Riley; Ms. Nyla Bonz; Murphy the Kanga-poo; Sumo; Frieda & Daisy Chains; Day-Z & Callie; Rosie; Rose; Augie Doggie; and Max von Sydow (the Belgian Prancing Dog): You have awesome families. I'm thankful they let me share my time with you.

To all of my students (past and present!) who took a training class, disc dog class, or found a way to get active with your dogs: Good job! Thank you all for submitting photos for this project, keeping me up to speed with your dogs, and touching base from time to time. I love hearing from you! This book is for you.

Tallulah the German shepherd: We never met, but if it wasn't for you, your owners and the court battle in Somerville after the attack, this might never have been written. This book was too late for Rocco and his owner—and for you and your family—but I hope this little book does its part to make sure that no other dog in Somerville (or any urban center) has to go through what you did. I'm so very sorry for everyone involved in that case and I wish you and your family (and Rocco's family) that time can heal these wounds.

R.I.P. Zeppelin and Samwise. All these years later and I still miss you both.

Lastly, to my departed friend, Sadie J. Dogg. You were everything in a dog I never, ever, wanted. There was no way I was going to get a puppy, a long haired dog or a herding breed. I certainly didn't want a dog with "issues." I just wanted a normal dog to go running with and maybe break the social barrier to meet people in my neighborhood. Yet I walked out of the Franklin County Animal Shelter in Columbus, Ohio carrying a 4-month-old, long haired Border collie puppy who had puppy-herpes and an insatiable drive for herding pinecones. For a dog that hated adolescent boys, black people, winter attire, statues, helium balloons, costumes of any sort, other dogs, the radiator turning on, and anything that looked like a weapon (which really put a damper on my fencing career), things worked out. You were my dedicated co-pilot and spirit-animal for twelve years. I couldn't have done any of this without you. I'm so deeply sorry for some awful mistakes and a large learning curve on my part; many of the mistakes are outlined in this very book. I did the best I could for you, and I promise that the dogs we have after you will have it better because of what we learned together. I promise to remember that when working with students. This book, some friends we've made, and being able to teach canine disc as part of my *actual job* (a profession I absolutely adore) would likely not have happened without your insistence on throwing the ball *just one more time*. You were an amazing companion and it really sucks now that you're gone.

They say that rescue dogs find ways to thank their owners for saving them. I don't know if that's true, but you did manage to pick Brian out of a crowd which seemed to work out favorably, and we're still married, so thank you for hookin' a sistah up. I can say without reservation that you've been the best teacher and wing-pup. I hope to live up to that with my students, my interns, and my staff. You did a good job, Sadie.

That'll do.

A Note on This Book

Now that I'm all done with this, it's important to note that my feelings on dog training have evolved over a period of 34 years. Those feelings have ranged from (and I'm embarrassed to even write this) biting dogs ears to prove I was 'alpha' at the wise-old-age of seven, to understanding that alpha is utterly and completely bunk.

I expect many things written in this book to change over time. That's the beauty of science—it's always proving new things. We once understood dogs were wolves, and now the science indicates that we really weren't correct. After training and working with dogs in both camps, I've come to realize that relationship based training just feels better. My feelings might change on some of the concepts, but in the last ten years I have always recommended puzzle toys, appropriate sports for an individual dog, and considerate off-leash recreation for dogs who can handle it. I don't see these recommendations changing, though the science might evolve to show some of my writing was short-sighted at the time. I hope it does! That would indicate we are looking at dogs as *dogs,* and we are doing more to help them in some meaningful way.

The best part about the theories and explanations in this book is that ideas evolve. Our dogs might not be in as dire straits a decade from now. That would be a wonderful thing. If the state of our dogs drastically changes for the better, it's still a good idea to always keep other people and their dogs in mind when you make decisions for your pet. Sure, your dog might still be friendly, and more "happy dogs" might cruise our city streets—but it would still be a good idea, even if the science proves new things over time, to keep your dog on a leash and be mindful of "the other guy." I don't think that will change, no matter what the science says.

We might have more access to tube-ties or vasectomies in our pet dogs going forward. This is getting more attention as I write this note. I didn't want to convolute my discussion earlier on spay and neuter, and I still don't think that this new take on sexually altering dogs will be any different from the advice I gave in the Spay/Neuter chapter. *Talk with your vet* if you have questions regarding new science, new techniques, new strategies, new everything for the health of your dog. The same goes for questions regarding vaccines…

…and anesthesia questions. There are many breed enthusiasts who still think that anesthesia will absolutely kill their dog. While that might have been more of a concern decades ago, anesthesia is much safer in 2015 than it was in 1950—so talk with your vet, and not your breeder, dog-walker or trainer about anesthesia, vaccines and health.

Overall, I hope that you take away just a few things from this piece:

- You are not alone in city.
- You are not alone in your position.
- There is help.
- You just need to know how and where to look.
- Our dogs are bored and need aerobic activity as well as mental stimulation for their health.
- Our dogs are bored and need aerobic activity as well as mental stimulation for our sanity.
- Genetics matter...
- ...but so does environment, and I would argue environment even more so.
- We all really want what's best for our dogs.
- We have to do better for our dogs.

I don't know if I will write another book, because this one had a very specific niche to fill, and from my vantage point as a professional in the city, it's a book that is needed right now. So maybe I'll see you again, maybe not, but remember this as a dog owner:

You've got this.

–M. McCue-McGrath

Resources

A list of recommended books, websites, and groups to help you get started.

Since this is not a book designed to train your dog, I felt it appropriate to put reliable resources here so you can find qualified assistance—or at least get you going in the right direction.

First, always, always know your veterinarian's phone number. Put it in your phone and even on speed dial.

Have access to the **poison control hotline**, know your local **24-hour animal hospital**, and if you are traveling with your pet, the nearest 24-hour animal hospital where you will be. It's better to know in advance where these are located and how to get to these places than during an emergency when adrenaline is high. It's best to always be prepared.

http://www.aspca.org/ has complete list of human foods and plants that are toxic vs. safe for our pet dogs. This website also has a fantastic behavior section, and where to get help for behavior issues.

Dogs in Need of Space (DINOS): A website dedicated to helping owners of reactive dogs gain confidence, advocate for their dogs, and get space for their dogs.

Fearful Dogs / Debbie Jacobs, CPDT-KA: Another fantastic resource for dog owners dealing with difficult questions and tough decisions.

If you are bringing a new baby home or are considering bringing a dog into a home with children, please bookmark the Family Paws and Living with Kids and Dogs websites. Get your hands on any books by Colleen Pelar.

John Bradshaw's book, *Dog Sense*, is the best writing on genetics, living with dogs, where our dogs evolved from, what they evolved to, and is another book that I can't recommend enough.

Patricia McConnell's books, writings, and blog are the go-to resource for students and trainers alike. She has easy to read, fantastic resources for many common behavior problems. They don't take the place of seeing a

191

certified professional, but they work fantastically in tandem with dog training. Her book *The Other End of the Leash* remains my cornerstone. It's the book that formed my feelings on dog training, and it doesn't really discuss dog training at all. It's required reading for my students.

Though she is gone, Dr. Sophia Yin's writings, behavior videos, posters, and dog-etiquette posters remain staples in the community. http://drsophiayin.com/ is her website. Her team continues to educate dog owners, trainers, and veterinarians about dog behavior, techniques, and health. Her free downloadable posters are a resource I use daily in my line of work, and I recommend you look at her dog bite graphics, dog play poster, and kids & dogs handout.

Steve Dale is an animal behavior specialist that has made it his mission to stop "underemployment" in our dogs and cats. His podcast, books, and column are digestible, easy to read, and very helpful for animal owners just starting with owning a pet who want to head off common behavior issues.

Victoria Stilwell's Positively network and YouTube Channel are great resources for learning to loose leash walk, stop door dashing, and other common behaviors that urban dog owners struggle with.

Slobbr is an app by my dear friend, Michelle Fournier. It's an app to help dog owners find dog friendly activities and shopping. Also included are pet friendly hotels, restaurants and hiking trails. If you travel the country with your dog, or just need something to do locally, this will help you remain active with your pet.

Other travel tips can be found on the CarTalk F.I.D.O page.

Find a Dog Trainer/Behaviorist/Consultant (not a complete list)
International Association of Animal Behavior Consultants: https://iaabc.org/consultants
Council of Certified Professional Dog Trainers: http://www.ccpdt.org/
Association of Professional Dog Trainers: https://apdt.com/trainer-search/
Karen Pryor Academy: https://www.karenpryoracademy.com/
American College of Animal Veterinary Behaviorists: http://www.dacvb.org/

About Melissa

Melissa McCue-McGrath grew up in an accidental dog sledding family in the small rural town of Washington, Maine, after her father inherited a dog sledding team. Melissa went on to get her degree in Psychology at Lake Erie College in Painesville, Ohio in 2003 after a failed attempt at getting a collegiate degree in equine sciences.

Immediately after graduation – and against better judgment at the time—she adopted a 4-month-old Border collie puppy named "Angel." After "Angel" barked at a group of African-American teenagers without provocation just 90-minutes after adoption, Melissa realized this both looked bad and wasn't an appropriate name for her new dog. She tossed names out into the ether for several hours, until her dog responded to one of them. "Angel" picked the name "Sadie" and from then on out, Sadie-Jane was by Melissa's side for twelve years. They competed in canine disc through the Yankee Flyers Dog and Disc Club out of Connecticut, and eventually became advocates for urban canine sports.

Though dogs are a huge part of Melissa's life, she also loves whiskey, her family and traveling whenever possible. She also really, really loves tattoos, hates pickles, and can't understand why cucumber is a necessary vegetable in vegetarian maki.

She's the Co-Training Director of New England Dog Training Club in Cambridge, MA—the oldest AKC obedience club in the country. She's worked with the team at NEDTC to continue changing the culture of aversive training techniques to positive reinforcement and considers working with this particular group her biggest achievement to date.

Melissa's been featured with Ollie the Flying Boston Terrier for PBS's Design Squad (a show that encourages kids to get involved in science and engineering). She has also appeared on numerous local news outlets promoting dog sports, training and local dog-friendly events. When not working with dogs, she makes handmade dog leashes for little dogs, and dogs that spend a lot of time off-leash.

She writes for CarTalk's F.I.D.O blog with her friend, Dr. Sip Siperstein. They love to laugh and educate. Though they are not Tom and Ray, they tip their hats to the style of Click-and-Clack, which is evident in their musings.

You can find Melissa blogging at http://muttstuff.blogspot.com, or some permutation of that if she ever grows up and gets her own domain. She teaches disc-dog classes in Reading, MA. She also teaches basic manners and puppy classes at Riverdog in Somerville, MA, at New England Dog Training Club in Cambridge, and sees students privately in their homes all over the metro-Boston region.

Unrelated to dogs, Melissa writes letters to her daughter, which can be found at https://letterstolittle.wordpress.com/.

Made in the USA
Middletown, DE
11 July 2020